Overshot

Overshot

The Political Aesthetics of Woven Textiles from the Antebellum South and Beyond

Susan Falls & Jessica R. Smith

THE UNIVERSITY OF GEORGIA PRESS ATHENS

A Sarah Mills Hodge Fund Publication

This publication is made possible, in part, through a grant from the Hodge Foundation in memory of its founder, Sarah Mills Hodge, who devoted her life to the relief and education of African Americans in Savannah, Georgia.

Athens, Georgia 30602
www.ugapress.org

Designed by Erin Kirk New
Set in Miller Text and Univers
Printed and bound by Sheridan Books
The paper in this book meets the guidelines for permanence and durability of the Committee on Production Guidelines for Book Longevity of the Council on Library Resources.

Most University of Georgia Press titles are available from popular e-book vendors.

Printed in the United States of America
24 23 22 21 20 P 5 4 3 2 1

Library of Congress Cataloging-in-Publication Data
Names: Falls, Susan, author. | Smith, Jessica R., 1971– author.
Title: Overshot : the political aesthetics of woven textiles from the Antebellum South and beyond / Susan Falls & Jessica R. Smith.
Description: Athens : The University of Georgia Press, [2020] | "A Sarah Mills Hodge Fund publication"—Verso title page. | Includes bibliographical references and index.
Identifiers: LCCN 2019033185 | ISBN 9780820356679 (hardback ; permanent paper) | ISBN 9780820357713 (paperback ; permanent paper)
Subjects: LCSH: Hand weaving—United States—History—19th century. | Textile design—United States—History—19th century. | Coverlets—Southern States—History—19th century. | Southern States—Social life and customs—1775–1865. | Museum exhibits—Social aspects—United States. | Aesthetics—Political asepcts—United States.
Classification: LCC NK8912 .F35 2020 | DDC 746.1/40437—dc23
LC record available at https://lccn.loc.gov/2019033185

ISBN 9780820357720 (ebook)

For Our Families

Contents

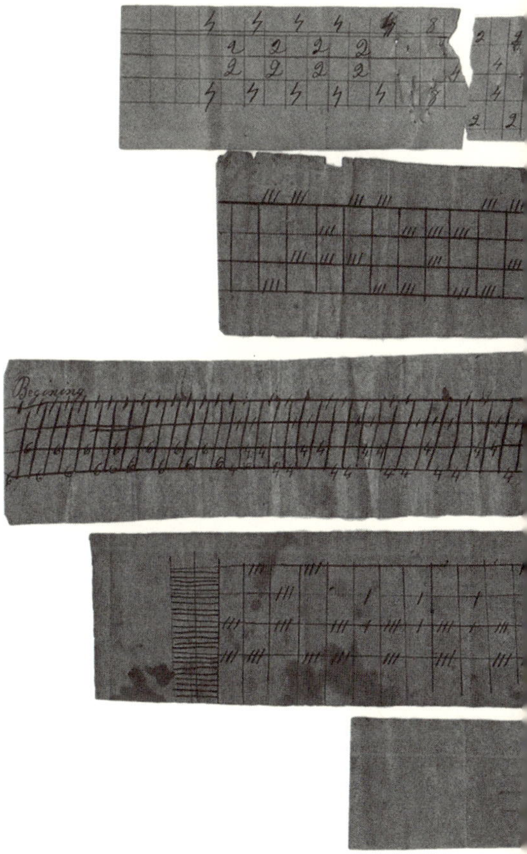

Illustrations

Figures

Plates

Color plates appear after page 52.

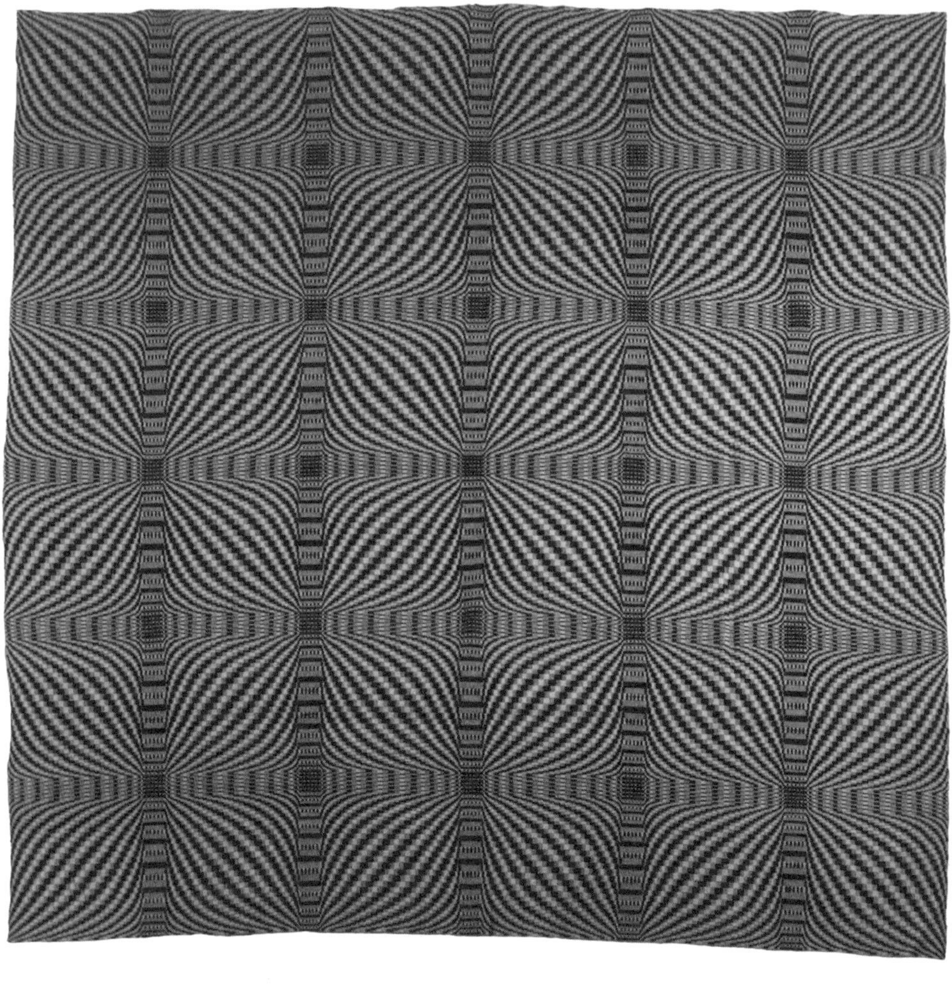

Figure 1 Overshot coverlet woven by Cassie Dickson (2012). "Double Bow Knot" pattern in cotton and wool. Photo by Bryan Stovall.

Preface

Woven coverlets have appeared in several guises within the history of folk textiles. Created on four-harness looms, coverlets made in the nineteenth-century American South typically featured colored wool and cotton threads woven into striking geometric patterns.

Although they are not as well known as other textiles and domestic objects (such as quilts or furniture), these "overshot" coverlets are significant examples of early American material culture. In addition to being pleasing to the eye and hand, woven coverlets indexed a variety of social, political, and economic ideas that have changed over time.

With these observations in mind, but never having seen or read about the history of woven coverlets as everyday goods made or used by enslaved Africans, we were intrigued when we saw a pair of them on display in 2012. Two overshot coverlets were exhibited alongside pottery, baskets, and two chairs associated with slave life at the Owens-Thomas House and Slave Quarters in Savannah, Georgia (see plate 11 and fig. 11). We would reconsider this exhibit many times over the next several years.

At first, we focused on trying to discover more about the provenance of these and other coverlets "said to be made by slaves." But over the next several years, the scope of our inquiry shifted as it became clear that we had stumbled on a set of aesthetic objects that were not only caught between art and craft but that were tracking over time as political objects, appropriated in a series of projects that included not only enslaved workers, but poor, rural mountain weavers and university-trained artists and craftsmen.

Overshot analyzes a series of coverlets, each one selected for its ability to epitomize a moment in history. These objects—representing antebellum slave and yeoman production, circa-1900 craft revivalism, or twentieth- and twenty-first-century artistic practices—index a landscape shaped by transformations in the cotton industry, commodity capitalism, aesthetic practices, and technological innovations, as well as by shifting racial and class divides.

As we worked through these materials, we noted provocative parallels between the historical circumstances and movements that encouraged women to weave coverlets and current DIY movements and populisms that characterize today's bifurcated political landscape. In the past, artists and craftsmen have registered dissent and offered alternative ways of being through their work. We see contemporary craftivists drawing again on the history of overshot as inspiration for making much-needed visionary material culture.

Our aim is not only to cast into relief the often-overlooked skill and creativity involved in creating woven coverlets, but also to show how these erstwhile domestic, utilitarian objects explode the art/craft dichotomy and belong to a rich narrative of art historical forms. We accomplish this by showing how geometric overshot coverlets can be understood in relationship to the global economy (especially with regard to labor, raw materials, and technology) and within politicized cultural movements. In the same way that the political can only be explained by identifying its aesthetic components (see Sartwell 2010), the aesthetic can only be understood by explicating how it is shot through, or *overshot* as it were, with the political. The woven coverlet *is* its aesthetic features *and* the politics that produced it. Neither the aesthetic nor the political is privileged: both have been necessary to the production, circulation, and interpretation of these objects.

Acknowledgments

Many people helped us to develop this book. Research for our project was funded by a grant from the Center for Craft, Creativity and Research, a Pasold Research Fund Grant, and a Presidential Fellowship from the Savannah College of Art and Design.

We also would like extend a very special thank-you to Dale Couch, who always encouraged us to continue digging, meeting with us on numerous occasions to discuss the development of the thesis. His encyclopedic knowledge about the decorative arts of Georgia in general, and of the legacy of the Jackson sisters in particular, proved invaluable.

Madelyn Shaw, the first textile historian we contacted when we started investigating provenance practices, helped guide our research; we are enormously grateful for her suggestions.

Results from a preliminary foray into the topic of overshot were presented at the 2012 Textile Society of America conference, where our paper was nominated for the Founding Presidents Award. The award was established in 2006 to recognize excellence in the field of textile studies; although we did not win the prize, just being a nominee gave us encouragement to proceed. We delivered other exploratory segments of this work for both the Seventh Henry D. Green Symposium of the Decorative Arts and the following (eighth) symposium at the University of Georgia in Athens. Symposia participants gave us momentum with their many insightful comments and hard-to-answer questions.

Feedback, reading materials, and counterexamples shared by scholars, collectors, curators, docents, artists, and weavers improved the book. Glenn Askew, Mack McFarland, Michelle Gillespie, Erick Montgomery, Jan Heister, Bonnie Carter, Rebecca Bush, Deb Wiedel, Susan Crawley, Melinda and Lazlo Zonger, Amanda Peck, Daniel Ackermann, Cathy Wright, Linda Eaton, Nancy J. Glaser, Anne Lewellen, Lindsay Pettus, Michelle Baker, Clark Johnson, Kathleen Staples, Andrea Feeser, Jill D'Alessandro, Tania Sammons, Julian Brash, Jeff Maskovsky, Elan Abrell, Elsa Davidson, Pellegrino Luciano, Kathleen Curtis Wilson, Lynne Milgram, Erin Martineau, Katherine Rapkin, Megan Ave'Lallemant, Suzy and Robert Currey, and Paul Pressly—we thank you a thousand times over for your generous constructive criticisms.

Each and every weaver, keeper of family heirlooms, and collector who participated in the installation helped us to better grasp how overshot is understood and practiced today. Special shout-outs are due to Bryan Stoval, who literally went above to photograph all of the materials for *Fold Unfold*, as well as Cassie Dickson and Katie Glusica for their permission to depict work from our installations in this book. Beth Sale and Didi Dunphy believed in our project and hosted our installation and performance at the Lyndon House Arts Center in Athens. Fibers professor Robin Haller not only created a fascinating overshot piece that addresses the topic of immigration for *Fold Unfold* but also helped to bring the whole project to the Wellington B. Grey Gallery at East Carolina University, where Tom Braswell and ECU students helped with the installation.

Thanks to all of the knowledgeable librarians, archivists, faculty, students, and staff at museums, libraries, galleries, archives, and cultural centers across Georgia and South Carolina. We are particularly grateful for assistance from the staff at the University of Georgia, the Telfair Museum, the Savannah College of Art and Design (SCAD), the College of Charleston, the De Young Museum, the Cooper Hewitt, the Acacia Collection, the Smithsonian Institute, the Charleston Museum, the Textile Society of America, Drayton Hall, Magnolia Hall, Liberty Hall, the Woodrow Wilson Boyhood Home, Bulloch Hall, and the Georgia Archives.

Editorial staff at the University of Georgia Press helped us to transform our research into a manuscript. We are particularly indebted to our editor, Lisa Bayer. Deborah Oliver combed through a cowritten text, helping us to find our more unified voice. We appreciate the patience of the copyright team who helped us to navigate the world of historical image copyrights, as well as the artists, photographers, and permissions officers at museum and cultural institutions across the country who were willing to share their work with us.

Our colleagues at SCAD—among them—in no particular order, Liz Sargent, Sheila Edwards, Deborah First, David Stivers, Kate Newell, Lisa Jaye Young, Afshin Hafizi, Désiré Houngues, Randy Moffett, Mary Doll, Cayewah Easley, Tracy Cox-Stanton, Scott Singeisen, and Capri Rosenberg—listened to our ideas and cheered us on, as they always do.

Our families, including Dare Dukes, Zimri Dukes, Tallulah Dukes, David and Beth Lee, Lee Falls, Gene "Crusher" Falls, Tinka Falls, Katherine Falls Mengedoht, as well as Matthew Stersic, Kami Smith, Gene Boyd, and Carol Smith wove this book into our shared worlds. Of course, all errors remain our own.

Overshot

Chapter 1 Setting the Loom

In the decades preceding the Civil War, coverlets with both geometric and figurative patterns became increasingly popular in rural American households as the availability of cheap industrially produced cloth freed looms for more decorative projects (Marks 1996; Strickler 1987).

Woven coverlets have an instantly recognizable appearance. The colors and bold patterns look familiar to a modern eye accustomed to pixelated imagery. Wonderful examples of these historic textiles can be found in national collections, most of which contain domestic geometric overshot coverlets from northern and mid-Atlantic states, where professionals wove fancy and figured patterns in workshops with multiharness (greater than four) or more complex looms (such as the Jacquard loom). In the southern states, high-contrast geometric patterns woven on four-harness looms with an overshot patterning structure of plain cotton ground and supplementary wool weft predominated (see plate 1). These southern coverlets are the starting point of this book.

Although plenty exist, southern overshot coverlets have limited representation in national collections. Of these, very few are sourced from lower regions of the Old South. Of the sixty-seven coverlets in the textile collection at the Smithsonian National Museum of American History, for example, only a small percentage are overshot, and of these, only one has a solidly southern provenance.[1] Southern textiles are particularly interesting not only because of their unique role within a long legacy of U.S. textile production but because they are, at times, attributed to being woven and used by many different kinds of communities, including enslaved Africans.

Throughout the Georgian piedmont areas (the area between the low country and Appalachian Mountains), overshot coverlets are associated with antebellum yeomanry, a group of middling farmers who owned few if any slaves. The kinds of bed coverings used to stage yeoman house museums varies, but they are mainly textiles made at home, including patchwork quilts, coverlets, and counterpanes (solid-color cotton weaves). Textiles exhibited in house museums meant to depict wealthy Georgians, on plantations or in urban mansions, are markedly different.

Figure 2 In the center of this historic coverlet is visible a labeling system commonly used for donated coverlets. From the boyhood home of Woodrow Wilson, Augusta, Georgia.

Coverings used to stage plantation masters' sleeping spaces tend to be either chintz appliqué quilts (of polychromatic European and East Indian imported cotton prints) or white bedding (often stitched, knitted, or white-on-white woven counterpanes). These materials stand in stark contrast with the textiles used to stage slave quarters or children's sleeping areas. Here, the same kinds of boldly patterned woven overshot coverlets with undulating geometrics that appear in representations of yeoman's homes are present, suggesting a tacit ideology of equivalence operating for yeoman, children, and enslaved labor against that of white masters.

Coverlet exhibits tell us a great deal about ourselves today, especially with regard to our ideas about race, class, gender, the value of women's work, and the separation of private versus public spaces. As instances of a relatively mundane but nonetheless powerful and remarkably consistent expressive practice, these textile exhibition trends reproduce a version of southern history that not only fails to adequately represent slavery as an unmitigated horror but also routinely underplays the social, political, and economic roles of the yeoman.

Meanwhile, though historians have shown us that yeoman farming had wide-ranging consequences (including but not limited to extending staple production into the piedmont, Indian land dispossession, and class- and race-based struggles between frontier settlements and coastal elites), this fact has been underplayed in both popular culture and academic research, sidelined by the historiographical binary of planter versus slave. Perhaps we should not be too surprised to learn of an elision of the middling classes in tourist sites devoted to pre–Civil War life since stories about the yeomanry and their material culture (still) tend to excite neither the praise nor the pity of planter and enslaved populations.

Folksy woven overshot coverlets do, however, star in a popular narrative about the South after the Civil War and into the early part of the twentieth century. The strong aesthetic of the high-contrast, polychromatic, geometric overshot was taken up by craft revivalists and proponents of the industrial arts in a philanthropic gesture meant to save southern (particularly rural Appalachian) communities from poverty, urban migration, and factory work. To accommodate their objectives, revivalists reinterpreted the meaning of coverlets. They shifted away from the antebellum-era practice in which weaving and woven objects were symbolic of yeoman independence from global trade and northern industrialization, and they advanced an early twentieth-century view in which coverlets worked as traditional chic for an emerging U.S. consumer class. Here, the purchase of a coverlet was promoted as both charitable support of Appalachian women and an emblem of nationalism. Both historical iterations commemorate southern American heritage as white and northern European, but they do so by reflecting different political investments and circuits of display.

By the middle of the twentieth century, textile designers and artists began to experiment in earnest with overshot weave structures. Overshot is often taught in universities as a simple, dynamic pattern-making structure, but it is often divorced from historic coverlet semantics. The form, however, has made its way into contemporary white-box art spaces. Today, coverlets are simultaneously offered as artifacts of colonial white Americana while the variety of optically stimulating designs produced by its strikingly simple structure is used by both artists and craftsmen.

To unpack this legacy, this book discusses the placement of overshot coverlets in sites of slave and servant quarters, yeoman life, museums, art collections, and revivalist shops to better understand how contemporary artists position them within the history of southern material culture. We investigate the meanings of the geometric overshot coverlet with particular attention to how appearances become connotation (e.g., the coverlet is used at times to suggest a make-do hominess). Further, we explore the political aesthetic of overshot coverlets, by which we simply mean how objects are valued and viewed with regard to aesthetic characters (e.g., patterns, materials, craftmanship) over time. But we are equally interested in exploring how they exude and act as expressions, catalysts, or reflections of political agency and thus articulate and perform the larger political-economic contexts in which they are made, used, and circulated.

To examine this political aesthetic, we mean to align the materiality and appearance of overshot coverlets (as woven, geometrically patterned, colored cotton and wool textiles) with questions about who made them and why. For the historic coverlets, this requires understanding farming patterns across the South, from the subsistence farming and diversified plantings of smallholding agriculture in the Up-country to the Plantation Belt's reliance on staple crops, as well as cotton's role in early industrializing capitalism up through the globalized, neoliberal capitalism of today.

Throughout, we have followed Terrence Lee Kersey (2009, 2017) and many others in mapping the history of Georgia onto its five distinct physiographic regions.[2] The Sea Islands in the low country were a hub where global markets interacted with a plantation economy focused on indigo, Sea Islands cotton, and rice. The Pine Barrens, a wiregrass region stretching from Savannah to the Chattahoochee River, at one time covered all or portions of twenty-three counties, according to the 1880 U.S. census report on cotton production. The Plantation Belt is also referred to as the Black Belt, a term popularized by Booker T. Washington. This was the dominant area of cotton production, with a higher percentage of enslaved blacks than whites (Ferleger and Metz 2014, 18). The Up-country, or Upper Piedmont region, is hilly, broken terrain that has been marked by relatively small farms and semisubsistence agriculture as practiced by the white yeoman majority (Hahn 2006). Last, the Mountain region follows the Appalachian ridge from Pennsylvania to Georgia.

As a case study focusing on a series of representative coverlets between the early nineteenth century and the present, we hope to reveal, or "surface," as Susan Star (1999) describes it, an otherwise hidden dimension of domestic decorative crafts. In some ways, this is an ontological move: by refusing to cut material culture out of its ambient cultural context, we recast it as equally and necessarily aesthetic and political.

Our Approach

As an interdisciplinary project conducted by a fiber artist-scholar and an anthropologist, we brought together methods, theory, and styles of analysis from the fields of both anthropology and the fiber arts. As we have done together with public art and silk woven ikat, in asking what coverlets mean from a point of view that is both from and between two very different disciplines, we hope to shed new light on these underappreciated objects. We hope to contribute a fresh perspective on contemporary exhibition practices as they reflect on slave, plantation, and yeoman life in the antebellum South.

Collaborative writing is as challenging as it is rewarding. We did not always agree on how to interpret or analyze materials, and at times we wanted to emphasize different aspects of culture, meaning, or history. We occasionally disagreed about theoretical relationships or methodological practices. We wanted both to write together and to write independently.

On the other hand, forcing each other to explain terms of art, hashing out many possible interpretations before committing to them, and working together in shaping and streamlining our central purpose was not just stimulating and fun, but in doing so we forged a new path through the materials we gathered.

To reveal the cultural backdrops inscribed within coverlets and to show how aesthetic activities operate as part and parcel of larger projects, we took a three-pronged approach. We examined primary and secondary sources on southern coverlets. We examined accession materials and spoke with curators, collectors, and registrars. And, perhaps most importantly, we visited museums, plantations, and art galleries in and around the piedmont and low country of South Carolina and Georgia to see firsthand how overshot coverlets were bring presented. Our perspective on overshot weaving is thus informed by triangulating what we learned in interviews with our observations and historical research.

At times, the production and use of the coverlets we examined in these sites could be determined by provenance materials, but an important epistemological issue remained regarding the transformation of unverifiable family lore into documented history. Staff sometimes take at face value family stories attached to artifacts donated to museums or historical societies; this seemed especially true at heritage sites and house museums, but this dynamic also cropped up in reputable historic museums. While most of these institutions do not have textile scholars on staff, they also lack funding to hire external consultants. It cannot be discounted that well-intentioned donors may have inadvertently added to, subtracted from, or misunderstood family stories, which, of course, can change over time and with repeated tellings (not unlike a game of telephone). An example of the way that semantic shifts are brought to bear here is in the term *homespun*.

Madelyn Shaw, Laurel Thatcher Ulrich, and other historians have demonstrated that all fabric of colonial production, whether made by an amateur at home or by a professional for resale, was at one time considered "homespun." The term did not connote a lesser-quality good or something made in the house, but a textile with a domestic (North American) rather than foreign provenance (Ulrich 2002; Staples and M. Shaw 2013). Homespun played a significant political role in the American Revolution narrative, where women entered into nonconsumption agreements and participated in a homespun movement, spinning and weaving in their homes in reaction to the British Townshend Acts of 1767 and 1768. The revival of rural domestic production in the spinning and weaving arts provided a way for colonial women to demonstrate their patriotism though a commitment to independence and industry (Ulrich 2002).

These earlier connotations of the term *homespun* as domestic commodity could easily be lost on a contemporary nonexpert. In common parlance, a "homespun" textile becomes something made not in the colony but literally made in the home. But family lore is just that, and when taken as documentary rather than literary, it can become part of an untried but public history.

At times family stories reporting home production—for example, claims that cotton and wool were grown, dyed, spun, and woven at home—is reproduced on exhibition plaques as factual information rather than as part of an unverified (and at times unverifiable) accession story. Contemporary ideas about race and class impact the way these accounts are used in the reproduction of history, acting, for example, as parameters against which registrars and curators perceive family lore to be credible or not. Of course, material culture used by docents and museum staff to stage historical narratives both reflects and helps to create ideas about historical life, events, and people.

Despite the dearth of overshot coverlets of solid antebellum southern provenance in national collections, we found plenty of coverlets in archives, museum collections, personal collections, and in reconstructions of the period between the Revolutionary War and the Civil War while traveling the back roads of Georgia. While the volume of coverlets in these places suggested that they were as popular in the South as they were the North, we often found them rather unceremoniously folded in closets, stuffed under beds, secreted in chests and armoires, or stowed under furniture (unlike appliqué quilts or white work, which were prominently displayed).

This made sense once we learned what local collectors and estate dealers think about woven coverlets. One estate dealer told us that, "unlike quilts, I don't even accept coverlets. You can't give 'em away!" Meanwhile, the more we looked, the clearer it became that—like quilts, tapestries, and other expressive textiles so prized by institutions and the public alike—coverlet weaving has a venerable history and an active present, making overshot coverlets artifacts of critical art and art historical significance. Efforts to value and preserve what is left of them are sorely needed.

The hold of antebellum quilts on the popular imagination is reflected in well-known books like *Stitched from the Soul* (Fry 1990), *Southern Quilts: Surviving Relics of the Civil War* (Ramsey and Waldvogel 1998) and *America's Quilts and Coverlets* (Safford and Bishop 1987). As an entry point, these works also nod to coverlets. These and other popular texts frame rural heirloom weaving as exemplary of make-do resourcefulness, advance the notion that mismatched seams dispel evil spirits, and promote the myth of the quilt codes (see Tobin and Dobard, 1999). These ideas are then reproduced in institutional settings. The story in which quilts made by enslaved people are encoded with maps or other crucial information about the Underground Railroad has been rejected as utterly without basis by most scholars, though its popular appeal continues unabated, enhancing the value of quilts, especially those with even a very weak slave provenance.

Similar to the boldly patterned quilts identified in slave code stories, overshot coverlets have a strong aesthetic. But coverlets have never been the subject of such idealistic suppositions (though the draft patterns appear both code-like and musical; one can easily imagine how they could be interpreted or used to inspire tales of subversion, mystery, or even romance). Their formal features also distance coverlets from the floral chintz appliqué quilts, crewelwork, embroidery, and tufting often associated with white elites at plantation sites. Formally, as well as semantically, coverlets inhabit their own category as objects that were circulated, highly valued, and promoted as public symbols by antebellum yeoman communities. Thus the coverlet form could not help but to serve as a node in which the aesthetic and the political became inseparable (a condition identified by Sartwell [2010] as artpolitical). But the relationship of antebellum overshot to art and design changed within postbellum nineteenth-, twentieth-, and twenty-first-century contexts.

Artpolitical

Makers have harnessed overshot's spectacular visual features. But crafted objects, like coverlets, should not be taken at face value (though its "face" has much to say). To know what it an aesthetic object *is*, it has to be "cross examined, along with the ideology of the artist and the political and cultural climate in which the artist worked" (Lampert 2014, 49). This cross-examination helps delineate the relationship between the aesthetic and political economy. Is craft an aesthetic form in which an alternative politics can be effectively expressed? How can art and craft be used to talk back? To what extent can "women's work" have a political voice? As Gyatri Spivak (1988) famously wonders for postcolonial subjects, can subaltern weavers "speak" through aesthetic production or do they end up unwittingly reinscribing the status quo? How are coverlet weavers like, or unlike, other artists and craftspeople such as rappers, Native American wampum producers, or Brechtian thespians? Can overshot work as dissent?

In considering these questions, we take as a starting point the fact that humans are meaning makers and object makers. Because of this, objects imbued with meaning by their makers are also interpreted, or "read," by others. These meanings may be sentimental, cultural, monetary, religious, social, or even moral. Gabriel Craig (2010) begins a history of moral imperatives in craft with a reading of the Venus of Willendorf (dated between 28,000 and 25,000 BCE). Craig offers the carved talisman as an early example of a crafted semiotic, widely believed to have invited possession through a cultural and spiritual relationship with fertility.[3]

Several thousand years later, Egyptians invested craft objects with psychological power and cultural beliefs. Wearing the symbols of deities (or their characteristic adornments) was believed to protect or enhance the wearer. For example, the Egyptian goddess Isis (giver of life, light, and Earth's protector, and in later periods, a fertility goddess) was characterized as a weaver and portrayed with a red sash around her hips. Artistic renderings of Isis up through the Roman period included this adornment. Even today, devotees wear a red sash, where red thread represents fertility, poetically described by Beverly Gordon (2014, 38) as the "transition point when nothing becomes something."

Symbolic elements have been integrated into other crafted objects not only to offer fertility or protection but also to help tell stories. Female weavers and their tools representing the standoff between Athena and Arachne are plentiful on Greek vessels (Barber 2006). On a larger scale, the Bayeux Tapestry, a 230-foot-long embroidered hanging stitched in brightly colored wool on linen ground, narrates the Norman invasion of 1066. The tapestry offers a celebration the Norman conquest while exquisitely depicting the gruesome details of war.

Although it was long thought that each panel of the Bayeux Tapestry was the work of nuns from a particular convent, with convents all across England participating, analysis by Alexandra Lester-Makin (2016) suggests that the consistency of its stitch work implies a different story of production: one group of specialists worked together in the same place under one manager or management team. Lester-Makin starts with the assumption that embroidery was a fundamental form of early medieval art, but considers how the act of embroidery enabled women to spiritually enter the sacred sanctuary space. Along with Craig's work on moral imperatives, we see how professional guilds and religious organizations have sponsored crafted narratives that linked symbols and skilled labor with moral conduct, if not political messaging.

Relatedly, and of especial significance to our work on nineteenth- and twentieth-century overshot weaving is Linda Stone-Ferrier's examination of the virtuous female spinners and yard winders represented in seventeenth-century Dutch painting (1991). Women spinning were popular subjects of oil paintings and woodblocks. Women at their spinning wheels were depicted as virtuous, whereas those embroidering and lace making were stylized as decadent and sexualized. The use of spinning to denote industrious feminine virtue would make repeated appearances throughout history, and indeed throughout the present book.

Of course, the meaning of an object or practice can veer away from the status of the maker to focus on the explicitly political, working as a critique of circumstances, policy, cultural values, or global dynamics. Nicholas Lampert (2014) shows that politically engaged art has been produced by individuals identifying as artists who were often trained in art school and otherwise showing work in museums and galleries. A well-known example of this is Picasso's antiwar painting, *Guernica* (1937).

Lampert also describes how politically engaged art has been created by nonartists participating in movement culture; here, individuals who do not identify as artists have employed visual means to advance political causes (Lampert 2014, ix). An example of this second class of politically engaged art is the AIDS Memorial Quilt.[4] In its first iteration, the names of family and friends lost to AIDS were written on place cards and taped to the wall of a San Francisco Federal Building. The resulting configuration, resembling a patchwork quilt, sparked one of the world's largest community art projects with clear political goals and messages.

Even more everyday objects that are aesthetic but not necessarily what most people might consider to be art, like flags, safety pins, diamonds, and hairstyles, can also be used to exert a political force. Artist Sonya Clark explores this idea in celebrating the talents of twelve hairstylists who manipulated Clark's own hair and stitched silk thread onto canvases. In Clark's (2015) own words, "the project breaks down barriers by crossing boundaries between hair salons and art galleries as sites of aesthetics, craft, skill, improvisation, and commerce."

Robert Sparrow Jones (2015) quotes Clark in his review of her work: "Hairdressers are my heroes. The poetry and politics of Black hair care specialists are central to my work as an artist and educator. Rooted in a rich legacy, their hands embody an ability to map a head with a comb and manipulate the fiber we grow into complex form. These artists have mastered a craft impossible for me to take for granted."

Here, quilt work and hair work by nonartists and artists operate within larger constellations of political activities. We see a third category of art-politically engaged makers and proponents emerging. Antebellum farm wives, teachers, revivalists, and Clark's hairdressers as makers and proponents who may or may not consider themselves as activists or members of a class or movement participate in a craft that exerts, wittingly or not, a political charge.

The mid- to late nineteenth-century British Arts and Crafts movement provides an historically instructive example of more explicitly political craft. Drawing on Pugin's elaboration of gothic style and Marx's critique of alienated labor, John Ruskin pushed an ethics of labor into craft production (Ruskin 1849, 1851). In his Arts and Craft movement, William Morris extended these ideas to promote ethical labor and social stewardship, political values if there ever were any, via the crafted object.

The introduction of the Arts and Crafts movement to the United States during the late nineteenth and early twentieth centuries by Elbert Hubbard (of Roycroft), Jane Addams (of Hull House), Candace Wheeler (of the Society of Decorative Arts), and others framed hand production as a rebuke to industrial manufacturing while advancing the artisanal ideal of labor. During the early decades of the twentieth century, the overshot geometric woven coverlet slid right into this line of thinking as a "revived" craft, having already operated during the mid-nineteenth century within a critique of class and industrial trade.[5]

Still, the relationship of art, and of aesthetics in general, to the political remains under-theorized despite the efforts to explicate the political dimension of aesthetic activity in the work of Marx, Ruskin, and Morris and then by Walter Benjamin and others associated with the Frankfurt School (see Corradetti 2002). During the 1950s and 1960s, French artists Guy Debord and participants in his Situationist Internationale looked for more innovative ways to use aesthetic means to revolutionary political ends. Today, Jacques Rancière (2010), Nicolas Bourriaud (2002), Crispin Sartwell (2010), and other scholars of political aesthetics have expanded our understanding of the relationship between the aesthetic to the political.

In *Political Aesthetics*, Sartwell (2010, 1) argues that while some but "not all art is political, all politics is aesthetic; at their heart political ideologies, systems and constitutions are aesthetic systems, multimedia artistic environments. . . . It's not that a political ideology or movement gets tricked out in a manipulative set of symbols or design tropes; it's that an ideology *is* an aesthetic system, and this is what moves people, attracts their loyalty or repugnance, moves them to action or apathy." He suggests that the political function of the arts—including various craft and design practices—is not merely a matter of manipulation and affect: the aesthetic expressions of a regime, or of resistance to a regime, are central to the cognitive content and concrete effects of a political system. Thus, to study politics is to study it within the context of a "multisensory surround or context" (2).

Sartwell's project recuperates art into a realm where power is explicitly being negotiated by showing politics as beyond the policies, platforms, declarations, laws, and other textual entities to which political analysis is often limited. Here, political systems are embodied in architecture, music, styles of movement, clothing and fibers, furnishings, and the graphic arts. It's not that political systems merely use these things as tools to gain loyalty or for propaganda; it's that a military junta, sharia law, and anarchism, for example, constitute "artpolitical" environments across media.

But his work is, in its essence, a study of the political by way of the aesthetic. In our study of coverlets, we propose a study of the aesthetic by way of the political. While we agree with Sartwell that not all art contains an explicit political message, we assert that all aesthetics are, nonetheless, political. And while we recognize the intention of the craftsman, we maintain that the meanings and consequences of one's work can surpass the maker's plans. There is always an excess to the aesthetic, and that excess addresses power in the sense that it indexes structural realities such as the circulation and access to raw materials, education, intellectual property, technology, ideology, value, production, commodification, gifting, circulation, meaning, and labor.

Our claim that even intentionally apolitical aesthetic objects are politically salient is essentially a semiotic position, that is to say, an argument about the *meaning* of objects. We can accept a maker's intention (or lack thereof) while maintaining the idea that there are additional levels at which an object like a woven coverlet should be interpreted. The best way to take seriously the craft of overshot weaving is to place it within shifting frameworks of production. Of course, the omnipresent background against which the American coverlet must be considered is the global cotton industry since there was a major expansion of the slave-powered cotton industry and industrially produced textiles in the decades leading up to overshot production in nineteenth century. It is here that overshot weaving has to be seen within an "artpolitical" environment, as Sartwell would have it.

From Homestead to White Box

Their highly recognizable aesthetic is partly a function of the way overshot coverlets are made. As Barbara Miller and Deb Schillo (2014, 23) describe it, the term *overshot* refers to designs made when a supplemental weft floats over more than two warp threads. Helen Bress (2003, 1) notes that it was referred to as "floating work" in early American texts. The basic weaving structure is a block twill, and when the twill line is expanded, reversed, and repeated in sequences, it creates geometric motifs; circles, tables, diamonds, crosses, and diagonal lines are the motifs used to create coverlet patterns.

A tabby weave is made with warp and weft threads; then a pattern floats over two or more warp ends to create the design. In many instances, a half tone is made with tabby and pattern in equal portions. This simple grid structure of overshot, like a binary code, allows for intricate permutations that historically were made using wool and cotton.

Cotton was king during the nineteenth century when most Georgian overshot coverlets were woven, but yeoman farmers shied away from the investing in risky market crops, instead focusing on self-sufficiency, raising livestock on unimproved and on improved land, growing mostly

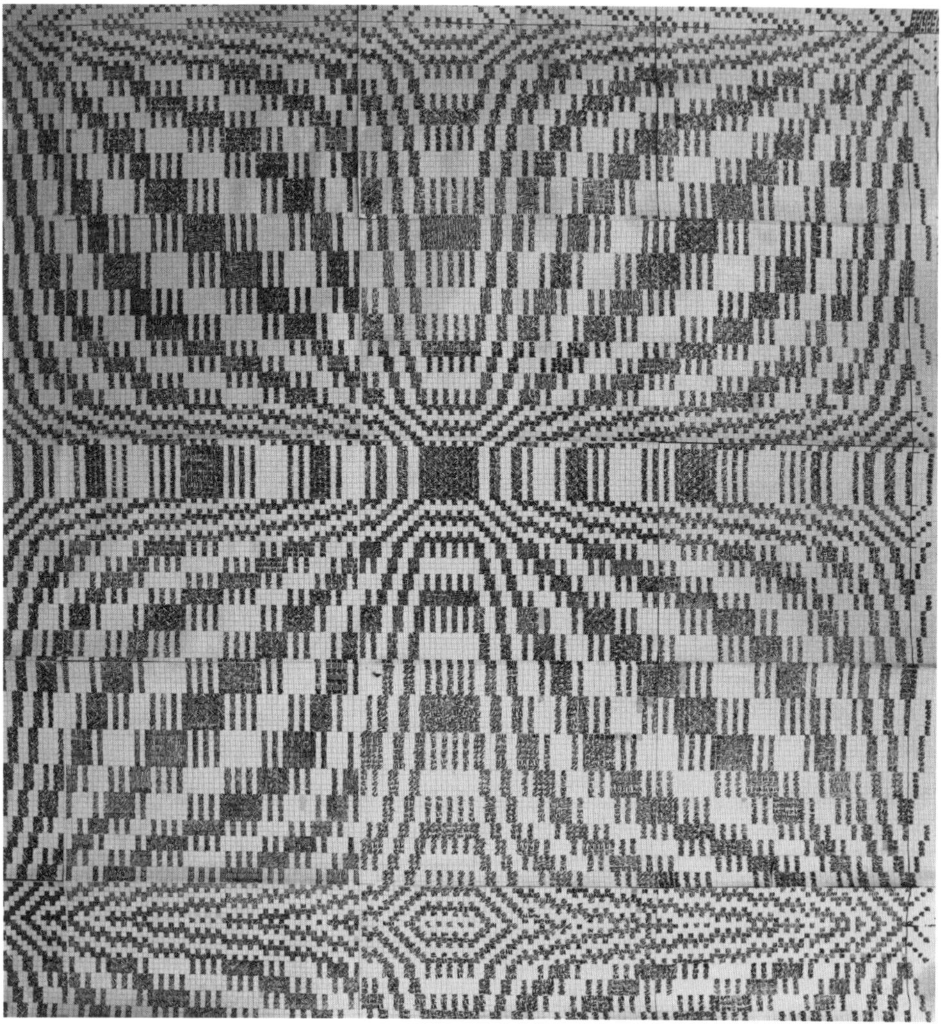

Figure 3 *Draw Down*, Katie Glusica (2016). Here a draft is "proven" or "drawn down" to paper to translate how the coverlet will appear when it is woven. The pixelation is symptomatic of the essentially binary nature of the weave structure.

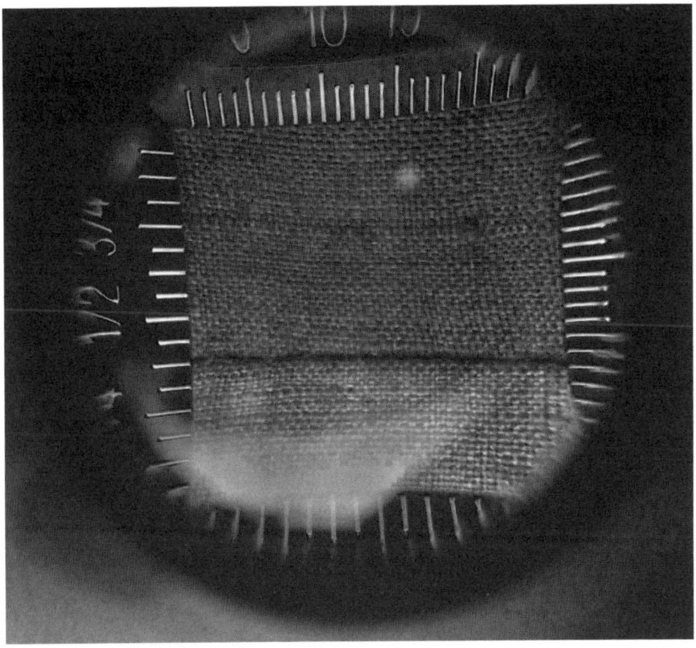

Figure 4
A magnifying loop aids in counting threads (yarn) in a weaving.

foodstuff and small amounts of cotton for personal use (Hahn 1985, 2006). And since most yeoman did not own gins or other new technologies seen on larger plantations, raw cotton was taken to a local gin and then a mill for processing. We have no way to trace the journey of any particular yarn in any specific coverlet, but the vast majority of coverlets we examined had a high number of ends, or warp yarns, per inch (EPI), a high number of picks, or weft, per inch (PPI) in the cotton ground, and the yarn was smooth and visually consistent, all of which indicate that the yarn was mechanically spun.

Over time, weavers had better access to commercially spun and dyed threads. Synthetic dyes were more readily available. Looms became more standardized as tools and production methods were mechanized. Handwoven objects were set against industrial standards, and the slight irregularities inevitable in hand production were read as signifiers of hands in direct connection to a maker's soul or, conversely, as a mistake (a reduction in quality). In the shift from heirloom object to commercialized commodities, coverlets made for sale or produced as prototypes for industrial production became simulated markers of old-timeyness or Americana.

Despite variations in the means of production, the basic configuration of the overshot coverlet has remained steady over time, operating as what Susan Star and James Griesemer (1989) have called a "boundary object." These are "objects that are both plastic enough to adapt to local needs and constraints of the several parties employing them, yet robust enough to maintain a common identity across sites. They are weakly structured in common use, and become strongly structured in individual-site use. They may be abstract or concrete. They have different meanings in different social worlds but their structure is common enough to more than one world to make them recognizable, a means of translation"(393). Star and Griesemer outline a typology of boundary objects including repositories, ideal types, coincident boundaries, and standardized forms and describe how boundary objects such as museum specimens to maps to technological protocols operate (411). Since boundary objects are used by members of multiple communities, they are also flexible, capable of hosting each group's (potentially conflicting) concerns and interests.[6] The key is in recognizing that, as a boundary object, the coverlet form can be followed through time and across cultural and political domains where people use it to accompany and to accomplish different ends. In many ways, the object acts as an avatar for makers positioned within an ever-expanding world of commodity capitalism.

Unfolding

In organizing this book, we chose a strategy that would reflect our process of discovery, following the coverlet through a somewhat chronological trajectory. Having examined the coverlet in popular nineteenth-century exhibition sites in Georgia and South Carolina and alert to the broader implications of our findings, we then examined how coverlet weaving was taken up in the twentieth and twenty-first centuries. We examined how they were exhibited and used, but also how they were made, circulated, and interpreted. Our strategy was thus to fold and unfold each coverlet as it was folded and unfolded in the places where we found them, a metaphor we explored in an installation and performance held at the Lyndon House Arts Center in Athens, Georgia (fig. 5).[7]

Mining site visits and interviews, chapter 2 examines coverlets associated with slavery. Many antebellum museums and other historical

Figure 5 *Unfolding*, 2017 (Susan Falls and Jessica R. Smith), Lyndon House Arts Center. The *Fold Unfold* installation culminated in a public performance in which each column of stacked coverlets was dismantled, the individual pieces were unfurled, and then the coverlets were restacked flat.

displays, especially those that were curated and maintained by white nonspecialists, tend to focus on how planter families lived. We contend that placing woven coverlets in slave quarters as typical, everyday goods is a provocation when one considers that other items of material culture (such as furniture, clothing, ceramics, and blacksmithed goods) that slaves had a hand in creating (or created entirely) are generally placed in the planter house to suggest how planter families lived rather than put in slave quarters to suggest what enslaved people designed or produced.

Meanwhile, it has become standard practice for reputable museums to acknowledge that most craft objects were likely made by an enslaved hand. But part of the challenge in using textiles to stage slave life is that cloth definitively known to have been made and used by slaves in their own quarters is scarce. Items that have been passed down by slave descendants tend to be small and easily transportable, whereas coverlets are quite large, approximately 80 by 88 inches.

Staff at slaveholding house museums we visited were unable to say whether the bedding used to stage the slave quarters could be traced to a slave or whether there was direct evidence of slave weaving. In a few instances, staff were able to share some information about coverlets' provenance; they had either been selected from general collections attached to the sites or purchased by staff for display.

Explicitly questioning the practice of presenting coverlets as typically made and used by enslaved Africans should not be viewed within the legacy of taking credit away from slave craftsmen, a practice with a long history tied to racism. We are, in fact, deeply invested in accurately locating enslaved peoples and their handiwork in the many spaces from which they have been absented.

It is well documented that slaves participated in the manufacture of cloth, which would have included coverlets, especially during the late eighteenth century and then again during the Civil War (when access to goods of all kinds, including textiles, was severely restricted). But there is little historical support for the idea that slaves were weaving coverlets for their own use between 1820 and 1861. Research focused on the period prior to the 1820s would likely portray a more inclusive landscape of weaving, and possibly a more widespread use of woven goods.

In historical displays, white work (e.g., a white-on-white coverlet) is often attributed and used to stage elite white spaces, while polychromatic coverlets, when they are used in antebellum sites at all, are relegated to the sleeping spaces of children, yeoman, and slaves. We contend that these exhibition practices unintentionally reproduce another kind of racism, one related to whiteness as a racial category stratified by class.

Since many people know little about coverlets or about the yeoman connection, those charged with designing exhibitions or with staging living quarters have mistakenly identified overshot patterns and materials as being outside of the categories of fine textiles (like appliqué quilts or embroidery) typically used to stage planter spaces. Without knowledge of coverlet history or the relationship they had to yeomanry, stagers apparently have drawn the conclusion that slaves must have made them or at least used them. And, during the early twentieth century when middle- and upper-class white families were donating their old overshot coverlets to institutions, there was little understanding of a landed (yeoman) farm class in the antebellum South operating outside of the plantation class. This practice of framing overshot as a slave practice may have later been exacerbated by representations in scholarly work focusing on the handicrafts of the enslaved and their connections to West African textile practices in which geometric coverlets are pictured side by side with quilts and other slave-made textiles (see Fry 1990; Vlach 1991).

When comparing reportedly slave-produced coverlets with textiles woven in West Africa, Gladys-Marie Fry and other scholars used visual affinities as the basis for comparison rather than the structure of the weaves. Doing so resulted in their incorrect assumption that the coverlets were made by slaves, as were the other textiles, including quilts. But a meaningful comparison between woven cloths must take into account the technological differences between the types of looms that weavers used and consequently the structure of the resulting cloth (details in chapter 2).[8]

Exhibitions are essentially pedagogical: they shape the way we think about antebellum slave, yeoman, and plantation life, which in turn shapes how we think about the present. Although by displaying these objects exhibitors may have intended to promote beautiful, skilled slave-made material culture, exhibiting coverlets as slave goods using weak or no provenance made a visual argument that reproduces dichotomies—for example, rural versus urban, primitive versus sophisticated, homey versus sparse, art versus craft, and of course, black (and not-quite-white) versus white—that needs to be problematized.

In contrast to the faint evidence that coverlets were everyday material goods for enslaved peoples, there is abundant support for widespread, routine production, circulation, and use by the yeomanry, a heterogenous group of white farmers who owned few if any slaves. Chapter 3 examines coverlets in period, art, and house museums associated with yeoman, as well as accession records, event spaces, and provenance practices. We found that antebellum coverlets made by the yeoman refracted shifting, and often times contested, ideas about the kind of nation the United States was and what it could (or should) become.

That chapter also focuses on the period between 1820 and 1860, when both plantation and yeoman women had access to imported goods, and when political and economic conflicts between the planter and yeoman classes were emerging. Textile production changed again during the Civil War, when commodity distribution was curtailed.

Chapter 4 tracks the life of yeoman women like the Jackson sisters, who were living in rural Georgia before, during, and after the Civil War. We place the sisters and their coverlet within a larger political-economic context in which they were struggling to carve out an existence. Caught between planter and poor white classes, the yeomen of Georgia and South Carolina enacted a Jeffersonian spirit of independence and self-reliance prior to the Civil War. This dynamic offers a lens to look more critically at the process by which yeoman weavers were edged out of some historical narratives but romanticized in others.

A powerful version of southern history created after the Civil War depicted a (white) nationalist Americana that papered over the complexities of race, class, and regionalisms characterizing the peoples of antebellum Georgia. Revivalist movements operating inside of this context celebrated coverlets as authentic emblems of folk Americana, rooted in Northern European weaving traditions, industrious domesticity, and innovative self-sufficiency. Here, coverlets were promoted as both real craft and as collectable folk art, but proponents of these movements also acted to capture weavers into wage labor, commodifying the fruits of their artistic production. We argue that until the antebellum white farming families of the U.S. South (that constituted the majority of the population) are more realistically included in representations of the region, the romanticized binary narrative depicting a world of wealthy planters and their well-adapted, content slaves (as depicted by the Lost Cause narrative recently explored in rich detail by Kytle and Roberts 2018) will never be adequately deconstructed.

Chapter 5 examines how coverlets were then brought through the twentieth and even twenty-first century in yet another guise. Lively debates about the differences between art versus craft influenced how this was done, especially when revivalisms began to split along the lines of those representing self-consciously modernist positions that advanced weaving as an art form ultimately to be viewed in a white-box gallery against "traditionalists" working with coverlets as utilitarian, bed-bound crafts.

Perhaps the best-known proponents of these two contrasting perspectives were Mary Atwater and Anni Albers. In many ways, their dispute reflected the bifurcating political and cultural circumstances of post–World War II America. Hobbyists and artists alike continued to align with traditionalist or modernist paradigms. Then, in the 1960s, the optically charged patterns of coverlets serendipitously aligned with geometric abstraction and op art movements. In the 1980s, when folk art, vernacular art, and outsider movements gained steam in the gallery scene, coverlets again became symbols of early Americana resourcefulness and rural independence.

Today, the trope of overshot weaving is positioned within yet another artpolitical milieu within the crowded landscape of modern homesteader, do-it-yourself, buy local, and craft heritage movements, each of which is a latter-day reincarnation of idealized yeoman independence. The contemporary version of optically stimulating design work can be seen in critical, exploratory interpretations by Allison Smith, Stephanie Syjuco, Rowland Ricketts, Josh Faught, Liz Sargent, Christy Matson, and other fiber artists.[9] In the world of gallery art, the function of the coverlet as bedding has been overtaken by its formal and semiotic features, its economic value a highly institutional affair. Keeping an eye on the contemporary arts as we explicate the political aesthetics of history shows the relevance of tracking the circulation of coverlets—and material culture in general by extension—as objects and as representations that define their makers and their users through particular investments.

We both create and instantiate ourselves in the world through our interactions with material culture. Our intention here is to present overshot coverlets not just as potentially beautiful objects, but as examples of material culture marshalled by different regimes of discourse. Tracing the shifting modes of meaning attached to the coverlet helps us to think and feel our way through past, present, and future conditions of making, interpreting, and being.

The final chapter reviews how the coverlet works as a free-floating signifier, morphing over time. We have outlined the transfigurations of meaning and use to shed light on cultural prejudices about makers and making, the role of material culture in producing and undermining ideas about race and class, and about what is art and what is folk craft. Our own visual contribution to debates about art and craft, urban and rural, old-timeyness and the contemporary, was an installation called *Fold Unfold*, in which we attempted to interrupt some of these well-worn dichotomies. *Fold Unfold* addressed some of the claims we make in this book, namely that coverlets are made using highly developed skills, that they are linked to the economic context the antebellum South, that they have been used to stage house museums in ways that edit the slave experience into a more palatable but historically flawed Early America, and that they continue to be productively revisited in a series of craft revivals and high-art contexts. Like a coin with two sides, coverlets are political objects with an aesthetic face. One feature could not exist without the other.

The gridded structure of the coverlet, a condition of its production that serendipitously maps beautifully onto modern digital realities, presents itself (today as it did historically) as a field for debates about infrastructure, conformity and dissent, the flattening of cultural differences, and political hegemonies based on class and race. In the final chapter, we continue tacking back and forth between the history of overshot coverlets and contemporary art and craft practices to demonstrate how the issues woven into these objects continue to animate the production and interpretation of material and political culture.

Ultimately, and perhaps inevitably, our foray into the world of coverlets unearthed many questions, which remain for the future to answer.

Chapter 2 Said to Have Been Made by Slaves

Coverlets that once played a part in the making of history are now used in the telling of history, but how and why coverlets are included in, or excluded from, exhibitions, art histories, and collecting institutions are important questions. Overshot coverlets are relatively easy to recognize because the mode of making them—using a supplementary pattern weft on a four-harness loom with locally available materials (yarn) and harvested or imported dyestuffs—defines their visual grammar. This grammar makes coverlets stand out from other kinds of bedding. Making a high-quality woven coverlet requires considerable skill and artistic vision, but unlike quilts and embroidered goods, there are few southern specimens in northern or national textile collections. There are, however, plenty of overshot coverlets in Georgia and South Carolina.

The two coverlets we mention in the preface were the first coverlets we encountered "said to have been made by slaves." They were displayed in the slave quarters at the Owens-Thomas House and Slave Quarters, which the Telfair Museum operates as a historic house museum. Built in Savannah, Georgia, 1816–19 for the cotton merchant Richard Richardson, the Owens-Thomas House was later bought by the planter-politician George Welshman Owens. The Telfair now presents the upper carriage house as one of the earliest examples of intact urban slave quarters.[1] Slaves here would have serviced the house, unlike enslaved people on rural plantations, where they would have also provided agricultural labor.

The exhibition label at the site mistakenly stated that the coverlets had been made on a Jacquard loom (a machine used to produce a different kind of weave, and not something most enslaved Africans would have had access to). Displaying the coverlets in the slave quarters as objects on loan from the Acacia Collection—whose stated mission was "to collect, research, preserve and exhibit selected artifacts created by African Americans"—gave the indelible impression that slaves typically made and used overshot woven coverlets as they did the baskets, chairs, and ceramic goods also placed in the room.[2]

Knowing the association of overshot with northern itinerant and yeoman weavers, we were surprised to see these objects here. We wondered if slaves routinely wove coverlets. Did they weave them for themselves? If so, how did slave-made coverlets end up in museum collections? And, if slaves did not weave coverlets for their own use but for their white masters, what were they doing in slave quarters? What kind of evidence could we find for slave-made or slave-used overshot? Would we find more slave-made coverlets on display in nearby museum collections?

What we discovered was that both attribution and representational practices regarding coverlets associated with slaves reflect a palimpsest of contemporary beliefs about enslaved Africans, domestic production, the yeomanry, plantation ladies, the value of women's labor, and pre–Civil War material culture.[3] In the past, and really as a way to mask the realities of the slavery system, material culture associated with slave life was erased from the museum landscape. And when slave craft was pointedly reinserted into revised histories of American material culture, it came alongside an emerging colonial revivalist make-do model. Coverlets smoothly fit into this paradigm.

Figure 6 Blue-White Cup and Saucer pattern woven coverlet fragment from the Charleston Museum. This fragment was anonymously donated in 1939. The accession card states that "the donor says this was 'made by slaves about 1839 on a southern plantation'" and that the coverlet was featured in an African American exhibit in the fall of 2003. Courtesy of the Charleston Museum, Charleston, S.C.

Aesthetic, Political, and Economic Artifacts

Influential nineteenth-century visitors from northern states often described the South as an exotic landscape consisting of the plantation aristocracy, poor whites, and an enslaved labor force. Fannie Anne Kemble's *Journal of a Residence on a Georgian Plantation in 1838–1839* (1961/1984) and Fredrick Law Olmsted's *Journey in the Seaboard Slave States; with Remarks on their Economy* (1856) are among the well-known published diaries by northerners. Best-selling novels like native Georgian Margaret Mitchell's *Gone with the Wind* (1936) along with Victor Fleming's (1939) film adaptation have also shaped the popular imagination of the prewar and postwar U.S. South, and thus the staging of history.[4]

But as Ethan Kytle and Blain Roberts demonstrate in *Denmark Vesey's Garden: Slavery and Memory in the Cradle of the Confederacy* (2018), the way slavery is remembered or concealed in southern tourism sites is as much a reflection of antebellum travel journals as it is the continuation of post–Civil War elite white southern ideologies. This is particularly true in terms of the persistence of the Lost Cause narrative. This is the idea that the cause of the Confederacy was noble and just, with northerners waging war primarily against the southern way of life, with an ancillary belief in slavery as a benign practice exerted on behalf of the enslaved (see Pollard 1867).

To document how coverlets are positioned today as aesthetic, political, or even economic artifacts in staged histories of enslaved peoples living in the antebellum South, we followed a popular tourist itinerary. We recorded the placement, appearance, and attribution of woven coverlets where we found them: along the coasts of South Carolina and Georgia, where slave quarters are sometimes an adjunct to rural plantation houses; at tourist sites in Atlanta and its surrounding neighborhoods, where urban history is presented; and in the museums of yeoman history in the cities of the Georgia piedmont, among them Augusta, Athens, Washington, Crawfordville, and Madison. Many of these yeoman sites are near the plantations where former slaves were born and lived—and later interviewed for the Works Progress Administration (WPA) Federal Writers' Project.

Woven coverlets in both house and museum exhibits and in museum collections were attributed to slaves in one of three ways. Attributions were at times explicit only in archival accession records not accessible to the public. In other instances, attribution was unambiguously communicated in exhibition texts directed at the viewing public. Or attribution was implicit: coverlets were placed in exhibitions alongside other examples of explicitly slave-made material culture, or shown in exhibitions meant to represent the typical slave experience.

It would be extremely difficult for visitors not to interpret these stagings as suggesting anything other than the idea that slaves typically made, owned, and/or used coverlets as they did the other items on display. Museums and historical monuments are powerful sites of ideological reproduction that command authority from members of the public. Visitors are therefore more likely to draw the conclusion that slaves made and or used these coverlets than they are to challenge museum authority on the staging. Even when no plaques or brochures spell out an association, the mere placement of these artifacts in an exhibit about slaves insinuates that slaves used woven coverlets in their everyday lives. An example of this perception is found in a visitor's online review of the exhibit at the Owens-Thomas House: "the carriage house stood as a stark comparison to the main house, but was every bit as fascinating to me, for it held furniture, stoneware jugs and woven coverlets used by the household slaves."[5]

A more verifiable staging might show the practice of weaving in association with slaves with no coverlets displayed as slave goods. Slave labor was integral to the production of both cotton and cotton textiles, so the placement of the accoutrements of weaving—cotton carding materials, spinning wheels, and even looms—in locations inhabited by slaves may be merited, but the story being depicted is not always supported by the facts of history. The Callaway Plantation just outside of Washington, Georgia, offers one example: there is a small outbuilding filled with weaving tools, referred to as the weaving/ironing house, where slaves would surely have worked. At the Middleton Plantation near Charleston, a spinning wheel is on display in Eliza's House, and a stableyard workshop is designated as the "Textile Shop" (fig. 7).

But while an absence of evidence is not necessarily evidence of absence, we found no confirmation of weaving having been done by slaves at either Callaway or Middleton (although there are coverlets and looms in the plain folk buildings at Callaway to depict a yeoman aesthetic predating the planter period). Docents suggested that the Loom House at Callaway may have been a laundry hut, while guides (who expressed an

Figure 7 Spinning wheel in Eliza's House at Middleton Plantation, Charleston, South Carolina. Built in 1870 for freed men and women serving the Middleton family, the house is named after its last occupant, Eliza Leach (1891–1986). Eliza's House opened as a house museum in 1991; by 2000, Beyond the Field (formerly called African American Focus) tours originating from the swept yard were describing the freed slaves' labor and how they spent any free time once their tasks were completed.

interest in the craft of handweaving) at Middleton told us outright that weaving had never been practiced there.

If museum staff do not believe that slaves wove there, why display a weaving exhibit? If historical accuracy is not being served, what is? Maybe these exhibits are meant to refer to the existence of weaving in general, since slaves were forced to work not only as field hands, but also as carders, spinners, and weavers of cotton fiber. And of course, at times, slaves processed into finished goods the very cotton they cultivated, at times sewing into clothes the cloth they had woven.

Clothing the enormous population of slaves was, as Madelyn Shaw points out, an industry unto itself:

> Our understanding of the complex processes and systems required to clothe enslaved individuals in the early South must be gleaned from surviving letters, memoirs, extant objects, and other documentation. Enslaved workers usually received most, if not all, of their clothing as an allowance from their owners. Some owners issued fabric, expecting the slaves to cut and sew their own clothing; some plantation mistresses cut out or supervised the cutting out of garments from plantation-made or purchased cloth, to be made up by slave seamstresses or by the mistress and her daughters; and sometimes ready-made garments or pre-cut garment pieces were imported from northern manufacturers. (2012)

And, in addition to working with cloth for clothing, slaves were involved in the production of both plain and colored cloth of varying quality for both their own and for their masters' household use.

Voices of the Formerly Enslaved

Though not without its own problems, an excellent resource for learning about the relationship of enslaved people to woven cotton is the published collection of Works Progress Administration (WPA) narratives by former slaves. From 1936 to 1938, the WPA Federal Writers' Project hired out-of-work writers to interview surviving former slaves.[6] John Lomax, remembered today largely for his work as an ethnomusicologist, devised a questionnaire that the white field interviewers used to structure their interviews.

Written transcriptions of over two thousand interviews from former slaves in seventeen states constitute the massive compilation of first-person recollections that fills seventeen bound volumes in thirty-three parts under the title *Slave Narratives: A Folk History of Slavery in the United States from Interviews with Former Slaves* (Federal Writers' Project 1941).[7]

Volume 5, *Georgia Narratives*, is divided into four parts. The transcriptions pay particular attention to dialect and include rich contextual details as noted by interviewers. Only a small percentage of surviving ex-slaves were interviewed (creating a possible sample bias) and most of the ex-slaves that WPA teams interviewed were very young during the late antebellum era, well into their seventies, eighties, and beyond when the interviews took place in the mid-1930s. Time, as we know, can impact memory dramatically. Despite serious potential weaknesses in the data (the age of interviewees, the length of time that had passed, the fact that interviewers were white, the oddness of the interview context, etc.), the narratives remain useful, and when recollections of similar details appear again and again across interviews, we can have greater confidence in their veracity.

Many interviews in the Georgian ex-slave narratives contain mention of work in cotton fields and in cotton processing (spinning, carding, and dyeing), as well as references to both weaving and sewing clothing and other textiles, including coverlets.

These activities were mostly reported to have been undertaken by people other than the interviewee, and at times they were offered as memories of something someone else had told them about a third individual's activities. For example, in speaking of cotton fields and production, Amanda Jackson, born into slavery near Davisboro, Georgia, on the Calhoun Plantation, remembers that

> All of de slaves on de plantation worked in de fiel . . . on dis plantation dey raised practically everything—corn, citton, wheat, an' rye, an' a heap o' livestock, Dey wuz rusaiin' 'bout twenty-five or thirty plows all de time. . . . De white folks clothes an' all o' de slaves clothes wuz all made on de plantation, De marster's wife could sew an' she an' her mother an some of de slaves done all o' de spinning an' weaving on de place, I've worked many a day in de house where dey made de cloth at. To color de clothes dey made dyes out of all kinds of barks. If dey wanted yellow stripes, dey used dye made out of hickory bark. Dere was always plenty o' clothes fer everybody 'cause dey give two complete outfits two times a year—one in de summer an' one in de winter, Fer blankets we used homespun spreads. (A. Jackson 1941, 289–90)

As Jackson suggests, slave labor was crucial not only to cotton production, but to the considerable task of clothing and outfitting slaves with sufficiently warm bedclothes. And, of course, slaves produced cloth and clothing for others, so it's unsurprising that weaving skills and woven goods are depicted as valuable in these narratives.

Indeed, Isaiah (Isaac) Greene of Greene County, age eighty-one at the time of his interviews, remembers that his grandmother was an "extraordinary weaver," but he does not say what she wove. He does state that her skills made her esteemed and that these skills may have led to her being treated better than she might have otherwise been (Greene 1941b, 58).

Other former slave narratives confirm that sewing and weaving was a skill that afforded some slaves a bit of comfort. Easter Jackson of Troup County described how her mother received excellent care, never once being allowed to do any field work, and was kept at the "Big House," where she sewed for the household (E. Jackson 1941, 299).

Incredibly, slaves were at times engaged in weaving cloth for the Confederacy during the Civil War. Jane Smith Hill Harmon, born on the Smith Plantation near Washington-Wilkes, Georgia, was eighty-eight when she was interviewed. She reported that her mother "wuz a 'spert spinner an weaver, an' she spun an' wove things ter be sont ter de Soldiers in de War. I 'members dat, her a spinnin' an' dey say hit wuz fer de soldiers" (Harmon 1941, 101).

Relatedly, David Gullins (1941) states that his mother was a weaver on the Mappin Plantation; he describes start to finish cotton production, but the only end product he mentions is clothing: "Every slave had his task, and my mother was cook for the family and the weaver. All of the clothing was made on the plantation from cotton and wool. The cotton was carded, spun and woven into cloth and dyed. Likewise, woolen garments were made from the wool clipped from the sheep raised for this purpose. All these garments were made right on the plantation" (83).

In another account of weaving, Alice Green, who was a slave at Helicon Springs, told interviewers that

> slaves lived in rough little log huts daubed wid mud and de chimblys was made out of sticks and red mud. Mammy said dat atter de slaves had done got through wid deir day's work and finished eatin supper, dey all had to git busy workin wid cotton. Some carded bats, some spinned and some weaved cloth. I knows you is done seen dis here checkidy cotton homespun—dat's what dey weaved for our dresses. Dem dresses was made tight and long, and

> dey made em right on de body so as not to waste none of de cloth. All slaves had was homespun clothes and old heavy brogan shoes. (Green 1941, 33)

Green is describing cloth woven for the production of clothing. Telling a similar story, Dosia Harris, born in Greene County, Georgia, on the Downs Plantation told interviewers that, as a child, she "picked a little cotton up and down de rows" and describes the clothing given to her as "made out of coarse cloth wove on de loom right dar on de plantation. Some of dem dresses was red and some was blue. De cloth was dyed wid red oak bark and copperas, and dey used indigo what dey raised on de place to dye de blue cloth. De waisties was close fittin' and sorter skimpy skirts was gathered on to 'em. De underskirts was unbleached white cloth made jus lak de dresses only some skimpier" (D. Harris 1941, 107). Harris also described her family's bedroom in which quilts figure:

> De beds had high posties and some of 'em was nailed to de wall of de cabin. Dey didn't know nothin 'bout no wire springs den, and dey strung de beds wid heavy cords for springs. Dey made mattress ticks out of coarse homewove cloth; some was striped and some was plain unbleached white. Atter de wheat was thrashed evvy year de fomans tuk der ticks and emptied out de old straw and went and filled fem wid new wheat straw. Wisht I had a nice fresh made wheat straw mattress now. Us had plenty of good quilts for kivver. (105)

Although the term *kivver* (cover) appears in several narratives, few formal details were ever offered. Elisha Doc Garey of Hart County, Georgia, describes what his family used for sleeping on Joseph Glover's Plantation: "Us lived in log huts. Evvy hut had a entry in de middle, and a mud chimbly at each end. Us slept in beds what was attached to de side of de hut, and dey was boxed up lak wagon bodies to hold de corn shucks and de babies in. Home-made rugs was put on top of de shucks for sheets, and de kivver was de same thing" (Garey 1941, 2).

So, Garey, Harris, and others report weaving, as well as having and using textiles, but they only mention clothing, cloth, shoes, rugs, and quilts when they name a specific type of textile. Garey, for example, states that after the surrender Yankee soldiers took the plantation's beehives, wrapping them in "quilts."

There were no mentions of slaves making or having overshot textiles in the WPA Georgia volumes, although there are mentions of white masters having coverlets in other volumes, including the following from

Arkansas. Ex-slave Ida Rigley says (1941, 43) that "when the white folks had a wedding it lasted a week. They had a second day dress and a third day dress and had suppers and dinner receptions about among the kin folks. They had big chests full of quilts and coverlets and counterpanes they been packing back. Some of them would have big dances. A wedding would last a week, night and day." This suggests that coverlets were important to a dowry. Mollie Hardy Scott (born in Franklin County, Georgia, to Master Jim Hardy) explained (1941, 128) that "when the war was done he [her father] come and got me and we went to Barton County, Georgia. When I lef they give me my feather bed, two good coverlets and my clothes. White folks hated fo me to leave. We all cried but I never seen em no more." This suggests that she had received coverlets as castoffs after the war. Born just a year after the war, Hattie Thompson (1941, 315) makes an explicit distinction between how her enslaved mother made pretty white and colored coverlets and how she also quilted with close stitches and backstitches.

That Hattie Thompson's interview could be interpreted to suggest the co-creation of textiles, including coverlets, is instructive, since—unlike the clothing and decorative items produced in the household by plantation women with help from owned or leased enslaved labor—weaving in the mid-nineteenth century seems to have been relegated to outbuildings, spaces devoid of white woman's labor, at least in the Lost Cause narrative of the southern plantation wife as a lady of leisure.[8]

And, while it is possible that the term *quilt* in the WPA narratives was also being used to refer to coverlets, it is worth considering that the ex-slaves explicitly comment on sewing, quilting bees, quilts, and quilting in groups, whereas there is no mention of overshot, weaving drafts, designing or modifying patterns, loom accoutrements or setups, or anything else that might suggest the activity of coverlet weaving. On the other hand, in an interview with Tempie Herndon Durham, who was 31 at the close of the Civil War and 103 at the time of her interview, stated that

> my white fo'ks lived in Chatham County [North Carolina]. Dey was Marse George an' Mis' Betsy Herndon. Mis Betsy was a Snipes befo' she married Marse George. Dey had a big plantation an' raised cawn, wheat, cotton an' 'bacca. I don't know how many field niggers Marse George had, but he had a mess of dem, an' he had hosses too, an' cows, hogs an' sheeps. He raised sheeps an' sold de wool, an' dey used de wool at de big house too. Dey was

a big weavin' room whare de blankets was wove, an' dey wove de cloth for de winter clothes too. Linda Hernton an' Milla Edwards was de head weavers, dey looked after de weavin' of da fancy blankets. Mis' Betsy was a good weaver too. She weave de same as de niggers. She say she love de clackin' soun' of de loom an' de way de shuttles run in an' out carryin' a long tail of bright colored thread. Some days she set at de loom all de mawnin' peddlin' wid her feets an' her white han's flittin' over de bobbins. De cardin' an' spinnin' room was full of niggers. I can hear dem spinnin' wheels now turnin' roun' an' sayin' hum-m-m-m, hum-m-m-m, an' hear de slaves singin' while dey spin. Mammy Rachel stayed in de dyein' room. Dey wuzn' nothin' she didn' know 'bout dyein'. She knew every kind of root, bark, leaf an' berry dat made red, blue, green, or whatever color she wanted. Dey had a big shelter whare de dye pots set over de coals. Mammy Rachel would fill de pots wid water, den she put in de roots, bank an' stuff an' boil de juice out, den she strain it an' put in de salt an' vinegar to set de color. After de wool an' cotton done been carded an' spun to thread, Mammy take de hanks an' drap dem in de pot of boilin' dye. She stir dem 'roun' an' lif' dem up an' down wid a stick, an' when she hang dem up on de line in de sun, dey was every color of de rainbow. When dey dripped dry dey was sent to de weavin' room whare dey was wove in blankets an' things. (Durham 1941, 285–86)

Here, Durham vividly describes several steps in textile production at the Herndon Plantation of North Carolina: growing cotton, carding, spinning, dyeing, and weaving. She describes discrete rooms, possibly in the main house, but the rooms were set up as a large workshop or preindustrial factory. The "fancy blankets" she refers to as being woven by slaves alongside Mis' Betsy may be overshot coverlets.

The picture of slave textiles suggested in these interviews is somewhat congruent with that suggested by diaries of the era. In his autobiography, Frederick Douglass describes his experience of bedding and bed covers:

There were no beds given the slaves, unless one coarse blanket be considered such, and none but the men and women had these. This, however, is not considered a very great privation. They find less difficulty from the want of beds, than from the want of time to sleep; for when their day's work in the field is done, the most of them having their washing, mending, and cooking to do, and having few or none of the ordinary facilities for doing either of these, very many of their sleeping hours are consumed in preparing for the field the coming day; and when this is done, old and young, male and female, married and single, drop down side by side, on one common

> bed,—the cold, damp floor,—each covering himself or herself with their miserable blankets; and here they sleep till they are summoned to the field by the driver's horn. (Douglass 1845, 23)

Writing in 1838 from the Butler Plantation (a rice plantation) just south of Savannah, plantation mistress (and future abolitionist) Fanny Kemble protested (1961/1984, 102) that the slaves there "have almost all of them a rude bedstead, with the grey moss of the forests for mattress, and filthy, pestilential-looking blankets, for covering."

The sole mention of looms in Kemble's journal appears in the context of northern industrialists: "nor are we, here in England, without part in this tremendous sin and sorrow; we have persisted in feeding our looms, and the huge wealth they coin, with the produce of slavery" (236).

It is hard to reconcile depictions of bedclothes by writers like Douglass or Kemble with anything other than a kind of rough homespun. They are not likely referring to overshot coverlets, with their visually remarkable patterning and coloration. Neither the diaries nor the interviews seem to suggest that slave blankets had any special aesthetic or symbolic value.

On the other hand, the WPA narratives contain ample evidence that enslaved Africans participated in weaving cloth, at times in workshop-like settings. Accounts of slaves making coverlets turned up primarily in other kinds of documents.

Accession Records

Books and museum accession records contain accounts of slave-made coverlets. One of the earliest books on coverlet production, Eliza Calvert Hall's early twentieth-century *Book of Hand-Woven Coverlets* (1912), states that plantation slaves were often taught to weave coverlets, but Hall undermines this claim by noting that "time the destroyer" made finding facts about coverlets a serious challenge. Meanwhile, the book contains a photo of a colorful sample (from Warren County, Kentucky, during the early 1850s), allegedly made by a slave.

The veracity of accession records and diaries suffer from the same documentary vulnerabilities that make the WPA *Slave Narratives* and other books based on oral histories difficult to work with. These vulnerabilities include the age of a speaker, reliance on memory, oral reporting of family tradition, the use of second- and thirdhand accounts, the length of time

Figure 8 One of the first books on coverlet production was first published in 1912. This copy was purchased at a yard sale in Savannah, Georgia.

that has lapsed between an event and when is documented, the desire to create an impression, and the relationship of the speaker or donor to the interviewee (at times complicated by issues of race, class, and gender). But as with the WPA documents' narratives, credibility increases with the repetition of assertions across accounts.

In 1996, Mrs. Alton Hill donated a coverlet reportedly handwoven by a slave to the Roswell Historical Society (RHS) in Georgia. Accession documents refer to a family legend describing a Mr. Arrington. Following the Civil War, Mr. Arrington, who kept a "truck full of Confederate money which the children used for play money," was also said to have harbored "a deep hatred of 'Yankees' and blacks." His wife, a Mrs. Missouri (Williams) Arrington, gave this Arrington family coverlet to their daughter, Clara, who then gave it to her son, Alton Hill. His wife, Mrs. Alton Hill, donated it to the RHS archive (fig. 9). Accession documents state that "Missouri was 8 years old in 1853 when the coverlet was being worked by slaves of her family" and that "she remembered watching its weaving."[9]

This accession record is unusual because most accession documents simply claim slave production without elaborating or providing supporting materials. The names and voices of enslaved makers were absent from this and all other donor accounts we were able to examine.

When weaving labor was explicitly assigned in accession records associated with white families, farmers' wives were said to weave heirloom coverlets for their loved ones, or slaves were said to have woven them (at times, using cotton that was reported to have been grown, carded, spun, dyed, and spun on the plantation). At face value, the Roswell Historical Society accession card implies that slaves wove this coverlet for their masters. There is not the vaguest suggestion that the coverlet was intended for use by slaves, nor is there any intimation that a white mistress participated in overshot weaving.

Throughout our project, we tried to check assertions against additional sources and by considering the way that coverlets act discursively within broader representational practices—be they personal, scholarly, or institutional. In the case of the Arrington family textile, we examined 1850 census records to try to identify the enslaved weaver. But records of the Arrington and Williams families show that, during this period, Frederick Williams (Missouri's father) only owned one slave, a male.

This particular record does not necessarily negate Missouri's memory, as her family could have acquired additional slaves after the 1850 census

Figure 9 Missouri Williams's coverlet (1853), Roswell Historical Society (Georgia). Accession records state that it was donated by Mrs. Alston Hill in 1996 and "worked by slaves."

or leased enslaved weaving labor, or maybe the census was not accurate, but the records do strongly suggest that Missouri came from a yeoman farm rather than from a plantation.

Perhaps Mrs. Williams (Missouri's mother) also participated in weaving the donated coverlet, or maybe what young Missouri saw was plaincloth weaving (the WPA *Georgia Narratives* volumes contain accounts of planter-class women weaving cloth alongside their slaves). It is also possible, but not probable, that after the 1850 census was taken the family purchased a number of skilled enslaved overshot weavers, who then wove the coverlet.

In order to clarify the picture of southern coverlet production by slaves, it is crucial to recognize that different regions of the South had varying access to global markets during different times. In our study we kept three periodic distinctions in mind: The first period is weaving before 1820, when imported cloth was not widely available in those regions where we find the largest number of coverlets and the least number of slaves per household. A second period is weaving between 1820 and 1860, when rail transportation was emerging and a growing number of country stores linked yeoman farmers to global markets. It was also during this time that planters were accumulating wealth, consuming imported textiles, and purchasing plain cloth for an increasing number of slaves.[10] A third period is weaving during the Civil War, when imported textiles were again hard to obtain.

Prior to 1820, slaves participated in weaving textiles for planter and slave use. As Rebecca Felton's description (1919) of weaving on her grandmother's plantation suggests, slaves, who Felton refers to as "helpers," were tasked with producing cloth, including coverlets, for the well-to-do planter family.

Most enslaved people described in diaries like Felton's were not named by the diarist. And likewise, as Fry (1990) points out, while the mostly white families donating these materials to cultural institutions often provided abundant information about themselves, the slaves they say were involved in coverlet production are rarely identified. We did locate a single donor record that identifies a coverlet weaver attached to a named female enslaver from the pre-1820 era. A Mrs. Shumate, granddaughter of a slave owner, donated a coverlet to the Old Slave Mart Museum in Charleston, South Carolina, in 1948. The coverlet was reported to have been woven in 1800 by Mahala Clarke Knight's slave on the Laurel Hill Plantation in Virginia.

But starting in the 1820s, imported machine-made cloth became increasingly affordable and available, and the "fine" handcrafts such as embroidery and quilting became more popular with planter women in Georgia. Almost all of the samples we saw in Georgia and South Carolina are dated to this second period, between the 1820s and the Civil War. This is also the era of highest yeoman coverlet production in the South and when machine-made cloth was provided to plantation slaves because it was becoming less economical to have slaves fabricate their own textiles—cloth, clothing, or blankets.

Several of the southern coverlets (whole and fragments) in the Museum of the Confederacy in Richmond, Virginia, are attributed to slave production. But these slave-made items are said to have been made in the third period, during the Civil War, when imported goods were increasingly hard to come by. Slaves and non-slaves alike were weaving during the Civil War, and it is reasonable to believe that some slaves may have done coverlet weaving then, although it would have been much faster and easier to quilt or plain weave blankets in a time of exigency and soldiers preferred other kinds of blankets that were lighter and warmer (M. Shaw and Bassett 2012, 150).

We found no slaves identified by name in accession materials for coverlets woven, nor did any of the materials state that the coverlets had been used by slaves, during this latter period. But it is in the move from donor household to museum that anonymously "slave-made" coverlets take a step toward inclusion in educational exhibits about material culture or slave quarter histories, and secondhand and thirdhand family lore takes a step toward recorded history.

Discussions with curators and docents revealed that, in previous decades, donor statements about slave labor were often taken at face value, recorded on accession materials, and then used to make exhibition decisions. But before returning to the question of how coverlets are placed in spaces meant to represent slave life, let's review why coverlets were donated in the first place.

Both state and cultural institutions began the work of preserving regional heritage during the first half of the twentieth century. Middle- and upper-class families began donating old family materials to cultural institutions, with plantation and slave goods moving with volume into museums and historical societies.

At least one local collector suggested to us that the publication of the WPA *Slave Narratives* not only provided employment to out-of-work writers and artists and contributed to a growing interest in slaves' and ex-slaves' experiences. The project also encouraged the expansion of a market for antique goods in general and for slave goods in particular. Of course, this market summoned coverlets with a provenance involving slave labor into regional museums of Georgia and South Carolina.

The Charleston Museum has a sizable and well-tended collection of at least sixteen coverlets. We examined the accession cards, many of which indicate a white, non-slave weaver by first name or family name. Four of the coverlets are attributed to anonymous slave production. According to those accession cards, at least two of these slave-attributed coverlets appeared in a 1994 display of African American contributions at the museum.

The accession card for a fragment anonymously gifted to the museum in 1939 states only it was made by slaves on a southern plantation around 1839. The other fragment was donated during this same era by a member of the Towles family who stated that the coverlet was made on Martins Point Plantation by slaves.

Although Martins Point Plantation on Wadmalaw Island is a private residential community today, "in 1866, Daniel F. Towles, a Georgia farmer, purchased 1,200 acres of planting and marsh land that is now Martins Point."[11] The fact that Towles did not purchase the property until after the Civil War does not dismiss the claim that this coverlet was woven by slaves. Perhaps the coverlet was woven on his Georgia farm with enslaved labor, though the 1850 and 1860 federal U.S. Census Slave schedules do not list Daniel F. Towles as a slaveholder at those time (he could still have acquired slaves after 1860).

Given the considerable size of the Charleston Museum, four coverlets potentially made by slaves may seem like a small number. Previously, a larger collection of geometric woven overshot coverlets (whole and fragments) attributed to slave production in Charleston was held in the Old Slave Mart Museum (OSMM). Miriam B. Wilson opened that museum in 1938 at 6 Chalmers Street, on the site of Thomas Ryan's slave auction gallery.[12]

An Alabama newspaper quoted Wilson on her reasons for creating the museum: "I want to save things the Negroes were taught to produce while in slavery . . . some of the slaves, only just removed from savagery, learned to make some beautiful things and to make valuable contributions to the new society into which they were introduced."[13]

As her statements suggest, Wilson downplayed the idea that the planters or the plantation system were inhumane or cruel, "cast[ing] slavery as a labor system that rewarded the enslaved with the gift of civilization. Planters may have enjoyed the fruits of their slaves' labor, but they reciprocated by providing food, shelter, and housing for their charges. The artifacts that she displayed in the OSMM reinforced this narrative, offering tangible evidence of the lessons slavery has taught" (Kytle and Roberts 2018, loc. 4569, Kindle).

Despite Wilson's reprehensible attitude about slavery, her private, nonprofit museum was the first of its kind devoted entirely to the history and culture of enslaved African Americans. Over the course of twenty years, Wilson amassed approximately fourteen hundred objects attributed to the artisanship of the enslaved. Among these were a number of coverlets. The entire collection was eventually merged into the Acacia Collection.

In 2015, the Acacia Collection registrar was unable to locate for us the records for the coverlets they had loaned to the Owens-Thomas House. Instead, the registrar provided photocopied letters and file cards addressing the donation of other coverlets in the OSMM collection, which by then was also in the Acacia Collection holdings. Among these was a 1948 letter to Miriam Wilson from a Mrs. Feagin: I have in my possession a large bedspread, quite heavy, which I acquired from an [old?] Middle Georgia family [Singleton?] who [had?] a plantation near Hawkinsville, Ga., [before?] the war between the states. The cotton from which it is made was grown and picked by the plantation slaves, and spun and woven by slave hand labor. It is in a blue and white design, the dye being also a home-made product."[14]

Similar stories of production by slaves from raw material to final product recurred many times during our research, despite the facts that most cotton grown on plantations after the 1820s was not spun by slaves, and that making blue dye requires indigo (see chapter 3). The 1850 census for Hawkinsville lists enslaved people attached to a Singleton family, but Hawkinsville lies along the Lower Ocmulgee River, where the vast percentage of pre–Civil War white households were plain folk farmers who did not participate in big cotton until after the Civil War (Wetherington 2005). Perhaps this Singleton family had been a planter or yeoman family in which the wife wove this coverlet, with or without the help of an enslaved weaver.

Mrs. Feagin noted that an "an almost duplicate of this spread is now used on one [of] the beds at Liberty Hall, the home (now a shrine) of Alexander Stephens at Crawfordville." The pattern, Catalpa Flower, is well known and popular, so the fact that it is on a coverlet at Liberty Hall is not surprising. As far as anyone could tell us, the coverlets displayed on beds in the slave quarters, one of which has a Catalpa Flower motif, have been in the collection since it was staged by Daughters of the Confederacy more than sixty years ago. It is not a smoking gun, but it seems reasonable to entertain the possibility that Mrs. Feagin saw the Catalpa Flower pattern coverlet placed in the Liberty Hall slave quarters in the 1940s and then developed some assumptions about the pieces she had in her possession.

In 1953, Wilson received another donation for her museum, this time a coverlet fragment. The donor, a Mrs. Muschel of Yonkers, New York, wrote that the coverlet was woven on the Lovelace Plantation, near La Grange, Georgia, by slaves in the mid-nineteenth century using materials (indigo, cotton, and wool) grown on the farm. The slave schedules of 1850 and 1860 show that a Lovelace family in La Grange indeed owned many slaves.

This Lovelace fragment has several extraordinary features. First, the patterning, a simple variation on Monks Belt, has a dynamic op-art effect heightened by the use of a larger yarn size than what was typical for the period. Second, a fragment from the same coverlet and with accession records pointing to the same location is housed at the Cooper Hewitt, Smithsonian Design Museum, in New York (fig. 10).

Mrs. Muschel must have known she had something special to have donated fragments to two unaffiliated institutions (though she did not mention slave labor when donating the fragment to the Cooper Hewitt). The rarity of the fragment is confirmed in a 1955 letter to Wilson from a museum visitor: "Miss Wilson, I have been studying weaving here and abroad for the past twenty years and never have I seen this pattern before."[15] This pattern, striking as it is, would reappear in the context of unenslaved weavers and artists.

Figure 10 Detail, reproduction of the Lovelace Coverlet fragment, Cooper Hewitt, Smithsonian Design Museum. Woven by Jessica Smith, August 2016.

Figure 11 Blue coverlet from the Acacia Collection on display in the Owens-Thomas House and Slave Quarters, Savannah, Georgia (2012).

Wilson, who died in 1959, willed the entire OSMM collection, including its coverlets and the Ryan's Mart building itself, to the Charleston Museum. When that museum rejected the donation, sisters and OSMM supporters Judith Wragg Chase and Louise Alston Graves created the Miriam B. Wilson Foundation, raising money to keep the building and the museum collection intact. The OSMM reopened in 1964, and remained open until 1987, when the City of Charleston purchased the former Ryan's Mart building but not the collection.

Fate has ultimately not been kind to Wilson's collection. After the museum closed in 1987, Carroll Greene Jr. was selected to oversee the OSMM collection. An African American art historian who had visited the OSMM in 1968 while serving as an African American material culture fellow at the Smithsonian Institution, Greene had been instrumental in expanding the African American folk-art collection at the Smithsonian. In 1989, he merged the OSMM artifacts with his personal collection to create the Acacia Collection of African Americana, which was billed as "unlike any museum experience anywhere in the world, because each artifact was made and used by African Americans."[16] After Greene's death in 2007, the entire collection was recalled from loan and eventually auctioned in November 2017, including the coverlets.[17]

With no extant accession records attached to either of the coverlets displayed in the Owens-Thomas Slave Quarters on loan from the Acacia Collection, they were likely part of Greene's personal holdings, rather than in Wilson's OSMM collection. Until 2017, both were on display alongside other objects of material culture associated with enslaved artisans. One is a large-scale repeated bow-tie or tulip pattern with a smaller repeating lacelike motif in red wool on natural cotton ground (see plate 11). Despite the age of the coverlet, the red dye remains vibrant and vivid. The strength of the color may be due to the use of cochineal, what was once an imported and expensive dyestuff. The red coverlet is anachronistically hung unfurled on the wall so viewers can see the entirety of its intricate patterning.

The blue coverlet, which is in much worse physical shape, is displayed folded over a chair in a more utilitarian pose, alongside ceramics and baskets of many shapes and sizes (fig. 11). Although in the main house great care has been taken to represent the specific occupants of the house within particular time periods, docents reported that the Acacia Collection was staged in the slave quarters only to show a general picture of African American material culture from the slave era. The coverlets were auctioned in 2017, and the Telfair Museum restaged the Owens-Thomas slave quarters.

None of the donors in these examples indicated by whom or where the coverlets were used. In contrast, when fine embroideries, chintz appliqué quilts, and other textiles commonly associated with plantation mistress hobby crafts are gifted, they often are accompanied by specific documentation about their use by the white household.[18] And they are usually exhibited in white spaces, not in slave quarters even when described as slave assisted or even as slave made. This never occurs with coverlets, raising the question of whether those in charge of staging plantation spaces are attempting to right some of the historic erasure of enslaved skill. Or something else might be at play.

Celebrating African Aesthetics

Efforts to reinstate credit to the hands of enslaved labor have been supported on both regional and national stages. An enticing narrative linking enslaved peoples' material culture to African heritage emerged in the early and mid-twentieth century, became popular in the 1970s, was reinforced in the 1980s, and then was enhanced through the 1990s by some critical attention.

In "Negro Craftmanship in Early America" Leonard Stavisky argues (1949, 315) that "indeed, there is reason to believe that the Negro workers engaged with the Crafts while still on the continent of Africa" in prelude to a discussion about weavers in Sudan. This article predates his 1958 dissertation, "Negro Craftsman in Southern Atlantic States 1800–1860," cited by Fry (1990). Stavisky studied political science, not the decorative arts, but his work seems to have lent support to the idea that slaves brought with them from Africa weaving knowledge that they then applied to coverlets.

Reportedly slave-made objects began appearing in major exhibitions and scholarly texts representing African aesthetics and skills. Coverlets from the OSMM–Acacia Collection are featured in Judith Wragg Chase's *Afro-American Art and Craft* (1971), Middleton Harris's *Black Book* (1974), and Gladys-Marie Fry's *Stitched from the Soul: Slave Quilts from the Ante-Bellum South* (1990). These books, as well as those by John Michael Vlach (1990/1978, 1991) and other scholars, were instrumental in the movement to document skills that enslaved peoples had when they were taken from Africa. In celebrating an authentic lineage of African skill, these advocates sought to reframe slave goods and slave labor as important contributions to U.S. material culture.

Vlach and Fry have both argued that a bold geometric design style is indicative of an African heritage. Fry (1990, 10) lists Robert Horton's six design characteristics found in African American quilts, five of which could be applied to overshot coverlets: vertical strip organization, bold colors, large design elements, multiple patterning, and improvised rhythm (the sixth, asymmetry, can be found in the attachments of woven panels), noting that quilts ranged from those "with strong African influences to those that almost completely merge with European-American design decisions." Fry's "Quilts from the Quarters" chapter contains ten plates of slave-made coverlets, one of which is an image of the Lovelace fragment from the OSMM collection, that had been "made by a slave near la Grange Georgia" and that "served as bed coverings" (61).

Great care is required in using these characteristics to identify objects as the products of enslaved labor, since while many West African societies did and still do implement bold colors and geometric designs into textiles, so have many other cultures. Yet, during our visits, several docents cited the bold patterning of coverlets in support of a slave-made attribution. One museum curator explained to us that she had assumed a coverlet was slave made simply because it was blue.

The idea that Africans brought their weaving knowledge with them when they were transported across the Atlantic was reiterated on tours through slave quarters. For example, when asked if it was certain that slaves made the coverlets on display, a docent at a plantation site replied "yes, of course—the slaves brought their weaving knowledge from Africa." But loom-controlled structures, such as the overshot found in coverlets, exhibit patterns developed through written drafts and shaped by the constraints of the loom. In West African woven cloth, the pattern typically evolves in the weaving process through a handpicked supplementary weft, and though it is also guided by the grid and held together through its structure, various forms of what is often referred to as strip weaving produces cloth that is more free-form (see, e.g., kente cloth from the Ashanti and Ewe peoples).[19]

While the full history of North American overshot coverlet weaving has yet to be told, it is certain that craftspeople have used loom-controlled supplementary weft pattering with a plain (tabby) ground (similar to overshot) on simple four-harness looms in many parts of the world. The North American variation can be traced to Scandinavia, the British Isles, Ireland, and Germany before the early colonists crossed the Atlantic.

It is also well-known that slaves were brought to the low country for their regionally specific agricultural knowledge, and while some slaves would arrive with weaving skills, whether they came with weaving knowledge associated with a European overshot tradition is an entirely different matter. These certainties do not preclude enslaved Africans from participating in weaving overshot (and, obviously, some were taught to do it), but they do call into question the way that aesthetic features and the conflation of weaving techniques have been used to link overshot coverlets with a West African heritage.

Although it is impossible to definitively determine who made the coverlets held by the Acacia Collection and other institutions, we can examine how exhibitions—ensnared as they are with contemporary ideas about class, southern history, and the significant role of textile use and production therein—position coverlets within broader narratives of southern history.

Antebellum Exhibitions

We can examine the use of coverlets to represent antebellum life within larger ideologies related to whiteness, American Fancy, and the image of an antebellum South populated primarily by planters with their slaves and poor whites.

Work by Bridget Heneghan, whose work examines material culture in association with the production of whiteness, and other scholars helps to situate staged historical coverlets within several larger skeins of meaning. Heneghan (2003) analyzes the treatment of color, race, and gender in antebellum literature to reveal how whiteness operated through material culture as an avatar of race; white objects became desirable as symbolic shields against the blackness associated with slaves.

We too observed how white coverlets were valued differently in house museums, especially when the family was affluent and educated. The staging of the Washington Historical Museum in Washington, Georgia, is a case in point. In a bedroom there, several polychromatic coverlets were haphazardly folded and stored in an armoire, but a white counterpane (white-on-white coverlet) was prominently displayed on the master bed (fig. 12).

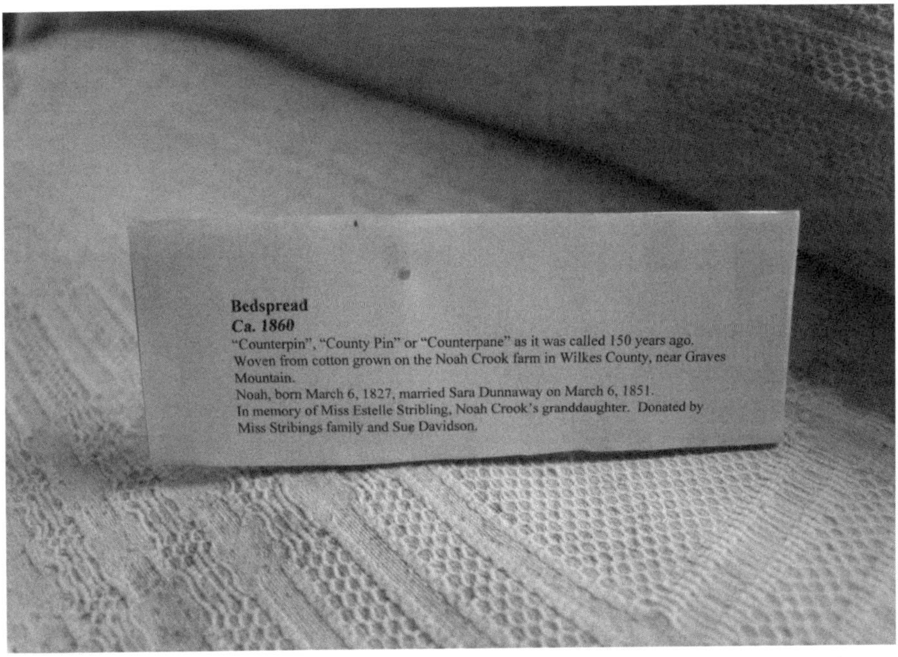

Figure 12 White counterpane in the master bedroom at the Washington Historical Museum. Reported to have been woven on Noah Crook's farm, Wilkes County, weaver unknown.

However, Sumpter Priddy (2004) suggests that colorful geometric overshot coverlets were part of a larger aesthetic trend. As Priddy defines it, American Fancy was about novelty, visual playfulness, and an earthy spirituality. In Priddy's vision of the late eighteenth- and early nineteenth-century interior, affluent households (in both northern and southern states) were textural, colorful, and full of patterning. Coverlets fit seamlessly into this vision (and in fact, his book contains a spectacular red overshot coverlet). On the other hand, the house museums we visited in Georgia strove to create southern charm à la *Gone with the Wind* through neoclassical design choices, imported furnishings, and all-white or chintz (floral) appliqué bed covers. This scheme leaves no place for the optically vibrant geometric coverlets that then go to the back of a cabinet, underneath the bed, or in slave quarters (fig. 13; see also plate 2).

We know that slaves designed, created, and used their own material culture, and they were given hand-me-downs or "cast-offs" from their white masters. For example, former slave Heard Griffin (1941, 75) stated

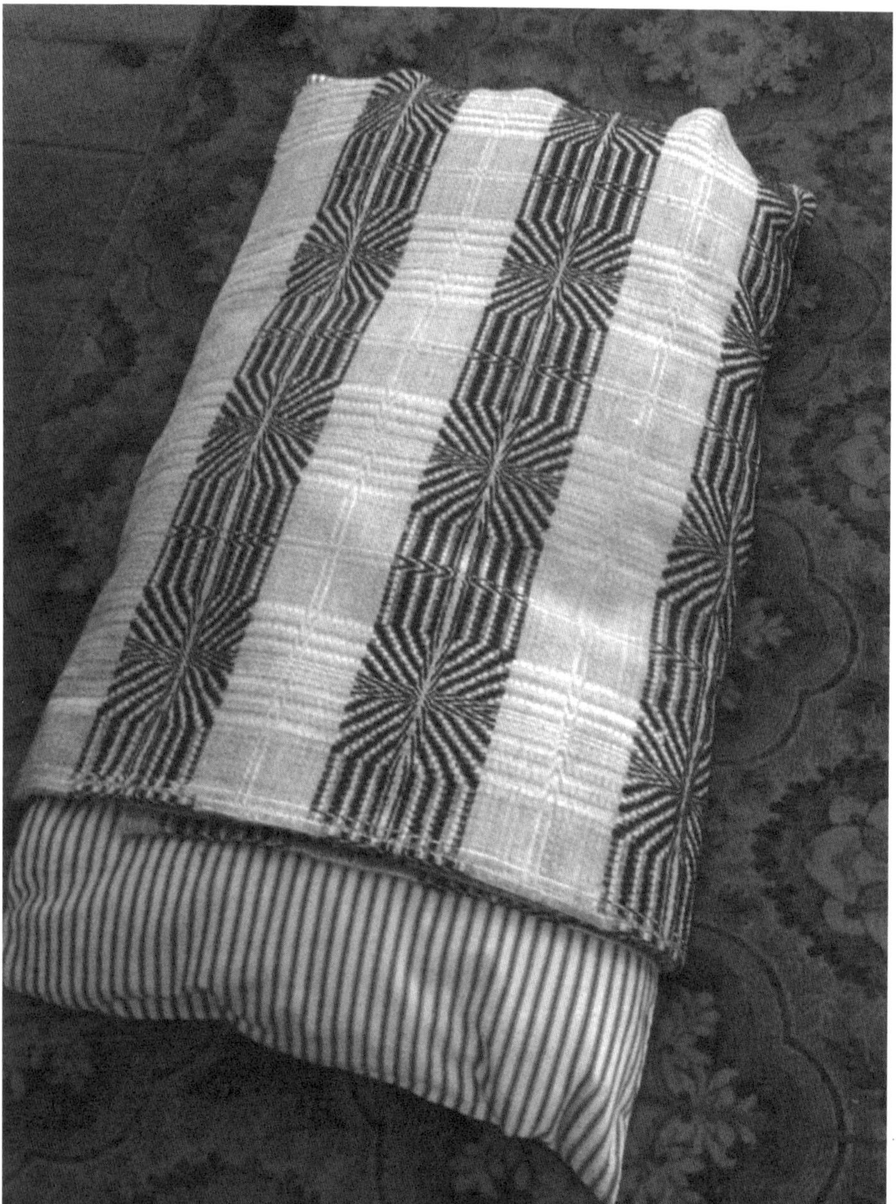

Figure 13 Coverlet on slave pallet under the bed at Bulloch Hall, Roswell, Georgia.

in his WPA interview that "discarded bed clothing was given to slave families on the Griffin Plantation."

Most exhibition texts in slaves' and masters' spaces fail to distinguish among the material culture made by and for enslaved peoples, goods made by slaves for their masters, and goods that slaves used as castoffs from their masters. In the case of coverlets, slaves could have woven or helped to weave coverlets for white masters but acquired them later for their own use as castoffs. But if slaves had a hand in making but not using coverlets, why are they exhibited as slave goods as if they customarily had them?

Taking this possibility a step further, even if coverlets were typically made by slaves for their own use, the question remains of how the white families who eventually donated them to cultural institutions acquired them. Here, slaves would have woven coverlets and used them in their bedrooms, but then a number of white masters would have acquired them and handed them down within their own families. The heirs would have then donated them to cultural institutions several decades later. White middle- and upper-class donor families could also have acquired them from former slaves after emancipation, but the question remains of how and why that would have occurred.

To date, no evidence supports either scenario. The dynamic driving the placement of these particular textiles in slave quarters despite such scant documentation may be a long-standing historical misconception, perpetuated early on by Frederick Olmsted and other visitors to the South, that the white South was dominated by just two classes, slave-owning planters plus the occasional farmer.

In contrast to the Olmsted version, Ann Patton Malone (1986) depicts a diverse society. She writes that the South Georgia piney woods farmer's simple economy and distain for "fanciness" in housing, dress, speech, and manners fostered a widely held misconception that only one class of southerner lived in the forests of the wiregrass region. These landless poor whites were characterized as malnourished squatters living in a sequestered backwoods existence, sustained by a few raw-boned range cattle, half-wild hogs, and several acres of stunted corn and sweet potatoes. As Malone discloses, this depiction was incomplete and, for the most part, inaccurate. In fact, South Georgia's vast pine forests harbored a lively cultural and economic society; and, at least through the 1880s and even past 1900, its people were remarkably self-sufficient, overwhelmingly landed, and freer from the genuine poverty experienced throughout most of Georgia during the same period (52).

Despite the pervasive southern stereotype of large estates with many slaves, records show that only a small percentage of slaveholding families fit that model. Historians following Frank Owsley (1949) began to correct the stereotype by writing about the yeoman, finding that most of the Georgian population were "middlin" yeoman (who owned few if any slaves) and those in the piedmont region lived in federal plain-style houses, rather than, as Olmsted describes them, log cabins of rough-hewed wood, with few rooms or amenities (see Vlach 2004; Olmsted 1856).[20]

Academic work has yet to dislodge the popular but misguided imagination that conjures a historic South populated only by planters, slaves, and underclass whites. Undocumented or only weakly documented coverlets donated to plantation collections or found folded up in house museum attics and chests therefore present decorators with an aesthetic quandary. Coverlets conform poorly to our notions about "fine" textiles associated with plantations (be they imported linens, quilts, or embroidered goods), and since in the still-powerful narrative of the historic South they cannot be conceived as associated with the poor, landless white, the only explanation left is that they must have been made by slaves. When faced with a lack of documentation and in subscribing to a set of nested dichotomies—art versus craft, fine versus folk, urban versus rural, sophisticated versus primitive, and finally, planter versus slave—those charged with staging plantation spaces have elected to categorize coverlets as rural, primitive folk crafts rather than with sophisticated fine, urban arts. Using this logic, they have used them to depict slave spaces.

Lives of the Rich and Famous

The use of coverlets in slave quarters at sites such as the Magnolia Plantation, the Woodrow Wilson House, and Liberty Hall does more than illustrate slave life, however. These coverlets also soften the imagined life of a slave, if not the idea of slavery itself, since these textiles add a touch of homey, decorative warmth. Mobilizing these same connotations—comfort, pleasure, and safety—for critique rather than a masking of racialized violence, both past and present, the artist Paul Rucker

Plate 1 Detail, historic undated coverlet from the collection of the William Roots House and Garden.

Plate 2 This upstairs bedroom at Bulloch Hall was staged by the Roswell Historical Society. The 1839 Greek Revival mansion in Roswell, Georgia, is also the childhood home of Mittie Bulloch, mother of President Theodore Roosevelt.

Plate 3 Jacquard coverlet in Woodrow Wilson's boyhood bedroom.

Plate 4 Overshot coverlet in Wilson's sisters' room. This is a uniquely large coverlet, and like the Jacquard piece shown in plate 3 is possibly of northern provenance.

Plate 5 Two overshot coverlets dyed with pokeberry. Top coverlet from the Lee family (ca. 1800s) of North Carolina (private collection).

Plate 6 *Some of Its Parts*, installation by Rowland Ricketts (2014), sound by Norbert Herbert. Indigo plants, Indigo-dyed cotton, Zuckerman Museum of Art, Kennesaw State University, Kennesaw Georgia.

Plate 7 Drayton Hall, Charleston, South Carolina. Founded in 1738, Drayton Hall is the nation's earliest example of fully executed Palladian architecture and its oldest preserved plantation house still open to the public (see http://www.draytonhall.org).

Plate 8 Bales of cotton wrapped in pink, outside of Athens, Georgia (2017), mark the current incarnation of the industry. Photo by the authors.

Plate 9 *Security Blanket (Drums of War)*, Allison Smith (2007), woven by Leigh Alexander. This coverlet is third in a series of five unique blankets published as a multiple by Dinaburg Arts LLC, New York. Exhibited in *Allison Smith: Notion Nanny*, University of California Berkeley Art Museum, curated by Elizabeth Thomas. Collection of Brooke Garber Neidich.

Plate 10 *Between a Rock and a Hard Place*, Josh Faught (2017). Photo credit: John Wilson White. Hand-dyed, handwoven hemp, Jacquard-woven cotton, and carnival flair on linen, 108 × 70 × 2 inches. A material mixture of high and low, hand-dyed yarn, the labor-intensive handwoven words found in the top corners of a 1982 edition of *Gay Areas* on the left juxtaposed with the much quicker jacquard-woven rendition of a red brick wall on the right. About this piece, Faught states that "the construction of identity is full of holes. It's full of a lot of inconsistencies. And it's full of a lot of competing impulses" (https://www.kqed.org/arts/13279959/bay-area-sculpture-right-now-josh-faught-weaves-monumental-cozies).

Plate 11 Red coverlet from the Acacia Collection, as displayed on wall in the Owens-Thomas House and Slave Quarters in 2017. Photograph by authors.

Plate 12 In 1937, Ruth Barnes painted this gouache and watercolor illustration of a coverlet woven by Mary Williams for the Index of American Design (now held in the Natural History Museum of Los Angeles County). "The Index of American Design was a depression-era federal work program in which artists recorded pre-20th century objects by producing painstakingly realistic drawings which at the time were more accurate than color photographs" (National Gallery of Art staff to Susan Falls, e-mail, January 29, 2019). See Mary Williams (object maker), Los Angeles Museum of History, Science and Art (object owner), coverlet, ca. 1937, watercolor and gouache on paper. Washington, D.C.: Index of American Design.

Plate 13 *Pattern Migration*, Stephanie Syjuco (2011). Commissioned by the Columbus Museum of Art. The fabric rolls and bags created for this exhibition are equally instructive.

Plate 14 Coverlet Fragment (USA), ca. 1850. Wool and cotton with continuous supplementary weft pattering (overshot) in plain weave foundation. H × W 85.1 × 42.2 cm (33½ × 16⅝ in.). Gift of Sara Mushel, 1956-173-1. Photo: Matt Flynn © Smithsonian Institution. Cooper Hewitt, Smithsonian Design Museum / Art Resource, N.Y.

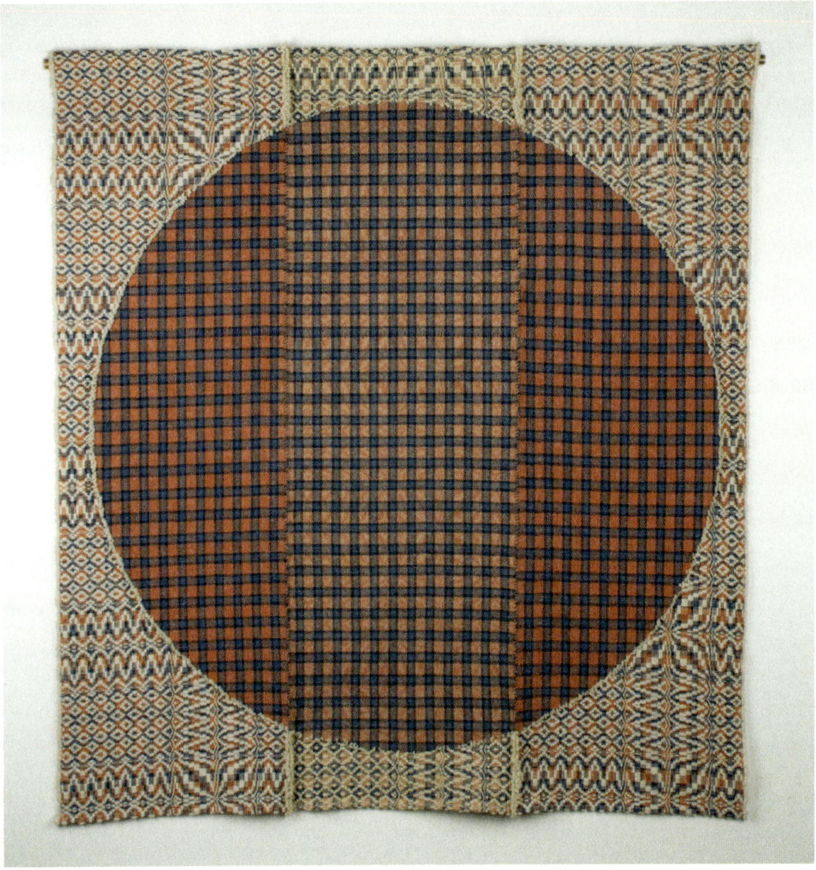

Plate 15 *Unbound*, series 3, no. 1, Rowland Ricketts (2018). Indigo and madder-dyed wool, undyed wool (2017–18), 61 × 68 inches. “Nineteenth-century American coverlets are both an embodiment and expression of our national identity. In red, white, and blue, these textiles visualized the young nation through emblems of state and the Stars and Stripes of independence. Looking closely, this American imagery was crafted by interweaving cotton—grown by slaves and spun in Northeastern mills—with local wools steeped in the indigo, madder, cochineal and brazilwood of colonial globalism. The material content of these textiles speaks much more directly to our nation’s history than any visual stories they tell. And yet we continue to believe in image over substance. *Unbound* is a series of experimental works created by weaving historical American coverlet patterns into a ground cloth based on the cotton plaids and checks that were integral to the triangle trade. Exposed for fading and selectively unwoven, these textiles are a meditation on the process of historicization, the formation of American identity, and the prevailing culture of the image” (Rowland Ricketts, 2018, “Woven: Unbound,” Ricketts Indigo, http://www.rickettsindigo.com/category/rowland-ricketts/woven/).

Plate 16 *Nostalgia for Inertia*, Liz Sargent (2009). Site specific installation at Pinnacle Gallery, SCAD, Savannah, Georgia. Original upholstery on furniture deconstructed and reworked utilizing various techniques including knitting and crochet.

printed images of lynchings and other killings on throws.[21] The effect is so powerful that York College of Pennsylvania took down its web announcement of the exhibit, restricted attendance to the York College community, and attempted to curtail the exhibit to two weeks rather than the planned seven weeks (Cascone 2017).

Museum vignettes of antebellum life could also be designed to function like this but typically do not. Not too far up the Ashley River from Charleston at the Magnolia Plantation, buildings that housed slaves are also staged with cozy-looking coverlets when we visited in 2012. This large plantation, founded in 1676 by the Drayton family, has five slave quarters. These slave quarters constitute "the Cabin Project." Each cabin (A–E) is meant to represent a different time period in African American history. Representing post-emancipation African American life in 1870, cabin D features a blue-and-white summer-winter coverlet made on a more complicated loom then the typical four-harness loom used for overshot (fig. 14). This weave creates a thicker material. The bedcovers here are exhibited along with other examples of material culture that would have defined freed slave experience.

Oddly, only cabin D uses material culture to illustrate everyday life (the other cabins are empty). Magnolia Plantation staff were unable to locate any documentation describing where this coverlet came from, who made it, who used it, or when it was woven, nor could they say who placed it in the slave cabin, when, or why. An unknown curator likely chose it from the general collection and placed it there, perhaps assuming it was a thing of slaves or newly emancipated African Americans, rather than a textile typically associated with the plantation owners.

It is also possible that the curator of cabin D chose this bedcover because it looked old-fashioned. The desire to achieve an old-fashioned look is how, according to the musings of one curator, an overshot coverlet landed at the foot of the "servants" bed at a house museum of Woodrow Wilson's childhood home.[22] Wilson's family occupied the Augusta home from 1860 to 1870 while his father served as minister at the First Presbyterian Church. The main house has been carefully restored by Historic Augusta to its 1860 configuration and furnished with many items original to the period of Wilson's occupancy.

Despite its billing as "depicting the life of the 28th President as a boy growing up in Georgia during the Civil War and Reconstruction," the

Figure 14 Cabin D, Magnolia Plantation, postslavery tenant cabin with summer-winter coverlet.

museum offers little information about the family's relationship to the enslaved. Given that Wilson came from a slaveholding family, his parents supported the Confederacy, and his father helped found the Southern Presbyterian Church in the United States (SPCUS) after it split from the northern Presbyterians in 1861 on the issue of slavery, this omission is a provocative oversight.[23] The "servant's quarters" is above the kitchen, sparsely furnished with spindle bed, side table, and a geometric overshot coverlet fragment (fig. 15). Docents indicated that the fragment came from the Ezekiel Harris House, an older historic house museum whose collection had been dismantled. The collection from the Harris House was turned over to the Augusta Museum of History in 2004. The bed now in the servant's room at the Wilson House had been in the Harris House main bedroom. When the collection was sorted and used to stage the Wilson house, staff felt that this primitive piece fit well with the 1797–1820 interpretation of the Harris museum but would have been too old-fashioned for the main bedroom in the Wilson home. It seemed better suited for the servant's room, where they likely had hand-me-downs. As best staff could remember, the coverlet on the bed came with the bedroom of the Harris House.[24] In this case, the coverlet is viewed and presented as a cast-off.

Similar dynamics power the expression of history at Liberty Hall, the historic Crawfordville, Georgia, home of Alexander Stephens, vice president of the Confederacy and then governor of Georgia. Here coverlets are displayed on the bed in the slave cabin, and on the two beds found in the cottage of former slaves, Eliza and Henry, who according to the tour guide "stayed on after the war to care for Stephens."[25] The park manager was unable to locate for us any records about the provenance of these coverlets. He assumed that they were part of the original collection present when the newly restored Liberty Hall and original twenty-acre A. H. Stephens Memorial Park was dedicated by the United Daughters of the Confederacy on July 18, 1935. We neither heard nor found any evidence to suggest that the bedcoverings had been changed since the Daughters of the Confederacy staged the rooms.

A small area at the rear of the house dates to the 1840s, when these coverlets were most likely woven. Between 1872 and 1875, Stephens replaced the main portion of the home with one in the big-house revival style of the day. He lived in the house until his death in 1883, when it was left to

Figure 15 Servants' bedroom in Woodrow Wilson's boyhood home, Augusta, Georgia. The coverlet fragment at the foot of the bed was previously displayed in a nearby museum.

surviving family members. In 1885 the property was purchased by A. H. Stephens Memorial Association and used to house the Stephens Academy until 1932, when the association deeded the property to the state, which eventually turned the property into the A. H. Stephens State Park.

The extensive Stephens property is considered "significant in *conservation, social history, and politics and government* as a major example of the type of work projects undertaken during the New Deal era" (original emphasis).[26] In the 1930s, Civilian Conservation Corps recruits restored Liberty Hall "for use as a house museum to illustrate the life of A. H. Stephens." The nineteenth-century servant house known as Harry and Eliza's House was also restored, as were several outbuildings, one known as Ellen's House. That building, likely named after Harry and Eliza's daughter, is now shown as slave quarters.

In 1952 a confederate museum was added on to Liberty Hall. Today it displays artifacts donated by the community, many of which are textiles, some with donor cards suggesting slave production, but with few details. In conversation with the park ranger there in 2016, we learned that the United Daughters of the Confederacy (UDC) were instrumental in the founding of Liberty Hall as a house museum and in collecting artifacts for staging the interior. This was not unanticipated, since after the Civil War white women with a keen interest in upholding the Lost Cause agenda took an active role in narrating the South in exhibits. Places like Liberty Hall were and remain sites where central tenets of the narrative are reiterated. So, it is important to look at Stephens's relationship to his enslaved house labor from the perspective of these UDC narrators (see Gardner 2006).

In 1910, UDC-approved journalist and documentary author of the southern experience Myrta Lockett Avary edited Stephens's dairy for publication (Avary 1910). In the introduction, she presents the house as Stephens's domain: "Liberty Hall was so named, Mr. Stephens said 'because I do as I please here and expect my guest to do the same.' . . . in the master's absence, as in his presence, open house was kept, his servants Harry and Eliza, doing the honours. Harry was Mr. Stephen's body-servant, butler, and man-of-affairs generally; Eliza, Harry's wife, was cook and feminine superintendent. Their children, Ellen, Fanny, Dora, Tim and Quin, engaged themselves about the place in work or amusement as convenient'" (87).[27]

Figure 16 The coverlet on display in Ellen's House (slave quarters), Liberty Hall, was referenced in Mrs. Feagin's 1948 letter.

The presentation of a benevolent master and his caring servants is as frequent in plantation and house museums around the South as staging with old-timey artifacts in living quarters. A travel guide, *Georgia: A Guide to Its Towns and Countryside* (Georgia Writers' Project 1940), written as part of the WPA program and sponsored by the Georgia Board of Education, describes the scenario on the Stephens' property: "One cabin, marked 'Eliza's and Harry's House,' and containing the old furnishings, recalls the story of Eliza, the cook, who was so much in love with Harry, the slave of a neighbor, that 'Marse Aleck' bought him for her" (508). While specific furnishings placed in the slave quarters have been removed since the WPA project was done (unlike the main house, where the furniture was described in detail), the general sentiment of the living space for the slaves as described in 1940 is consistent with what was visible in 2016.

This exhibit makes no explicit claims about slave production, but the coverlets are arranged alongside a spinning wheel and accoutrements of yarn production (but not weaving), strongly implying that they are slave goods: owned by slaves and used by slaves, if not also made by slaves.

Interestingly, Georgia Baker, ex-slave, stated in her 1938 WPA interview that she had been born around 1850 on the Stephens plantation outside of Crawfordville. She identifies Stephens as "de President or somepin of our side durin' de war" (Baker 1941, 42). In her discussion of textiles, Baker notes that women were carding cotton and wool: "Summertime us jus' wore what us wanted to. Dresses was made wid full skirts gathered on to tight fittin' waisties. Winter clothes was good and warm; dresses made of yarn cloth made up jus lak dem summertime clothes, and petticoats and draw's made out of osnaburg. Chillun what was big enough done de spinnin' and Aunt Betsey and Aunt Tinny, dey wove most evvy night 'til dey rung de bell at 10:00 o'clock for us to go to bed. Us made bolts and bolts of cloth evvy year" (41).

Here Baker seems to describe the production of cloth for clothing in a factory-style environment, with long hours punctuated by the closing bell. When she discusses anything that could be understood as a blanket, she calls it quilting and describes the collaboration that quilting allows (and that is impeded by the realities of overshot weaving). She says that "dey did quilt in de winter 'cause dere had to be lots of quiltin' done for all

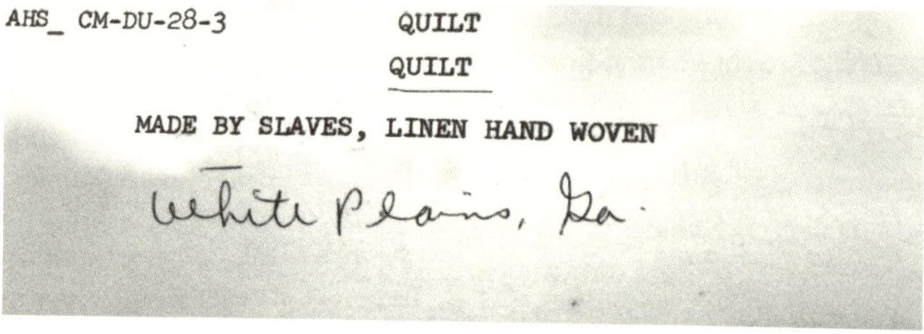

AHS_ CM-DU-28-3 QUILT

QUILT

MADE BY SLAVES, LINEN HAND WOVEN

White Plains, Ga.

Figure 17 Accession card for a quilt reported to have been made by slaves from handwoven linen. Confederate Museum, Crawfordville, Georgia.

dem slaves to have plenty of warm kivver, and you knows, Lady, 'omans can quilt better if dey gits a passel of 'em together to do it" (48).

Baker's transcribed interview does not relate whether slaves did or did not not weave or have coverlets. During the early twentieth century, when the story and representational practices of these spaces were being developed, coverlets were being marketed by revivalists as nostalgic remnants of a bygone era. But given Baker's account, the use of plaincloth or quilts to stage the bedding in slave quarters at Crawfordville might have been a better choice.[28]

That these coverlets hold considerable significance—regarding slave, master, and yeoman life alike—is without question. The presentation of a *Lives of the Rich and Famous*–style planter-class narrative is alive and well for tourists who come from all over the world to visit historic plantation sites to be entertained by learning how planters and slaves lived. Contemporary stagings of historical slave quarters reflect an ongoing devaluation of rural vernacular aesthetics and concomitant overvaluation of wealth, power, and celebrity. Per the remarkable consistency and persistence of the Lost Cause narrative, mentions of the yeoman in these settings are extremely rare (even though yeomen comprised the majority of the antebellum population).

Slave labor was fundamental to the workings of the southern economy, but currently available evidence suggests that slave participation in coverlet production between 1820 and the start of the Civil War was minimal. Yeoman coverlet production was, however, widespread, intense, and ongoing between 1800 and the rise of the cotton economy up through the Civil War. And in the decades after the Civil War the yeoman coverlet would be taken up as a celebrated emblem of American folk art with a dash of white nationalism (although its critical political underpinnings would be rewritten).

Exhibition designers have an opportunity to contextualize coverlets more deliberately. Even in plantation and urban locales, we can position elite and slave life with regard to the yeoman, a figure who has remained largely in the shadow of the spotlight on plantation families and slaves, but whose existence was fundamental to cultural, economic, and political dynamics of Georgian and South Carolinian society. To examine this unsurfaced history of the yeoman weaver, we need to look more closely at the coverlet itself, as well as at how different groups have appropriated overshot weaving in promoting different visions of America, history, and art.

Chapter 3 Plain-Style People

The written works and collections at museums shape how the viewing public understands the dynamics of history. A great deal has been written, and shown, about planter lifestyles and slave handcrafts. Although house museums, archives, and collections of the decorative arts from Georgia contain coverlets and other artifacts made and used by the yeomanry, these same purveyors of history are largely silent about these small or middling farmers constituting the region's white majority.[1] In this chapter we continue the work building on *Plain Folk of the Old South* (1949), in which author Frank Owsley calls on historians to develop the history of the yeoman.

Correctives like Owsley's have continued, albeit slowly, to chip away at the picture of the pre–Civil War South as essentially a class system of planters, slaves, and unlanded whites. Continued analysis of antebellum social strata will determine what criteria should be used in delineating the Yeomen from the Planter or Poor White (see Kersey 2017).

Acknowledging the significant inroads that Steven Hahn, Lacy Ford, Stephanie McCurry, and other scholars have made opening a space for yeomen in the history of the South, Kersey questions whether a seemingly arbitrary number of slaves (25) is a reasonable marker of yeoman or planter status, since the number of slaves was not always equal to the number of labor hours required. Instead, Kersey suggests that subsistence might be a more accurate kind of category to use; if a yeoman family is not self-sufficient, it might be sliding toward poor white status, but when the farm produces a surplus, the family may be transitioning to, or already is established as, a commercial farming family (Kersey 2017, 22).

Despite the relative lack of historical materials on yeoman women's aesthetic practices, the material culture of both enslaved and yeoman peoples is captured in books such as Gillespie's *Free Labor in an Unfree World: White Artisans in Slaveholding Georgia, 1789–1860* (2004), the Atlanta History Center's *Neat Pieces: The Plain-Style Furniture of Nineteenth-Century Georgia* (2006), and McCurry's *Masters of Small Worlds: Yeoman Households and the Political Culture of the Antebellum*

South Carolina Low Country (1995). These works provide an excellent foundation for the study of overshot.

The contributions of yeoman weavers are described in scholarship on antebellum textiles that focuses on the economics of production, plantation life, yeoman farmers, and the early days of the textile industry. Along lines explored in *Homefront and Battlefield: Quilts and Context in the Civil War* (M. Shaw and Bassett 2012), *The Southern Lady: From Pedestal to Politics, 1830–1930* (Scott 1995), and *Southern Women: Black and White in the Old South* (McMillen 2002), we cast yeoman women as accomplished artisans of the antebellum South. As we had done with coverlets associated with enslaved labor, we also took a critical look at museum documents. We found a well-documented, long-standing practice of artpolitical yeoman weaving.

Untangling Records

Staff at house museums associated with yeoman weavers aren't always able to provide accurate labels for textiles. Most places have neither textile curators on staff nor the budget to hire external experts. When consultants are employed, it is often only during an insurance appraisal.

In the case of the Jones family collection housed at the Colonial Midway Museum in Midway, Georgia, an insurance appraisal extended to decorative objects in the collection. In considering the coverlets, however, the appraiser appears to have relied on generalized texts about nineteenth-century coverlets. As a result, as with the misattributed loom description for the two coverlets at the Owens-Thomas House, handwoven geometric overshot coverlets displayed in the Midway Museum are described as having been made on Jacquard looms on the museum inventory.

In fact, overshot coverlets woven on four-harness looms use a block threading that is readily distinguished from the more complex Jacquard weave, in which each thread, triggered by a revolving punch card similar to that on a player piano, operates independently (see comparative Jacquard and overshot coverlets from the Woodrow Wilson boyhood home in Augusta, Georgia, in plates 3 and 4).[2] It is easy to imagine how an examiner not trained to identify different kinds of weaving structures and who was using images from books on nineteenth-century coverlet weaving for reference could easily mistake one weave for the other.

Most books on coverlets from the nineteenth century focus on coverlets woven by skilled itinerant artisans who learned their craft within a traditional master-apprentice relationship. By the middle part of the nineteenth century, these professional weavers were weaving "figured" and "fancy" coverlets on looms with a Jacquard attachment. Indeed, a number of Jacquard woven coverlets in South Carolina and Georgia museums are attributed to northern (presumably male) professional weavers.

Stories about itinerate weavers traveling the countryside and weaving for rural households were repeated in early American lore and texts on coverlets (Eberlein 1914, 416). How far, or how often, these weavers traveled is not well documented, but weaving families did set up shop in towns across the mid-Atlantic and northern states to take commissions for cloth, bedding, and linens (McCarl and Anderson 2002). Soon after the Jacquard attachment made its appearance in the United States in the 1820s, many artisan weavers adopted the new technology, advancing the popularity of figured and fancy coverlets across the northern states. No records indicate a similar practice of professionals weaving in southern states, a curious deficit that might be attributed to skilled artisans' unique opportunities to enter the planter class (Gillespie 2004).

Museum labels reflect when, where, how, or by whom a particular coverlet was woven as reported by donor narratives, which are then taken as fact. At times, these stories include second- or third-person accounts. In an attempt to reduce the uncertainty accompanying donor lore, we tracked down genealogical and estate records, and when lucky, gleaned input from local historians when we came across a coverlet donated by descendants far removed from the original date of production. For example, to learn more about the probable provenance of the Lovelace fragments from La Grange (Troup County, see chapter 2), we triangulated OSMM documentation with genealogical and census data. We also communicated with the Troup County historian, Clark Johnson, who shared documents about the Lovelace family that confirmed some details but posed a number of other questions about Muschel's Lovelace fragment donation.

What seems certain is that Mrs. Sara Muschel, granddaughter of Mrs. James Lovelace, donated a coverlet fragment to the Cooper Hewitt in 1956. Just one year earlier, she donated a strikingly similar fragment to Miriam Wilson's Old Slave Mart Museum along with a letter indicating that "these covers were woven by my grandparents' slaves at the Lovelace plantation near La Grange, Ga. As they moved from La Grange to Hamilton in their early married life, I am not sure where the weaving was done."[3]

In a 2013 e-mail exchange with Johnson, we learned that members of this branch of the Lovelace family were not only farmers but also skilled artisans who "operated a large leather tannery and manufactured boots and shoes as well as harness and saddles." Johnson's documents suggest that Muschel's grandparents (James Lovelace and Sara Jane Embry) married in 1853. Prior to their marriage, James Lovelace was listed in records as a farmer who lived with his brother, John, a tanner who had two slaves. But by 1860, as Johnson told us, "James and Sara had their own household (in which was found James' mother, Tabitha) and 2 slaves, and James was listed as a farmer while brother John M., still a tanner, had 8 slaves."[4]

Johnson noted that "in 1860, regardless of the occupation listed, all the brothers were connected with the tannery." He concluded by evoking a plainly yeoman-like image of the Lovelace holdings: "Troup County farms and plantations were self-sufficient and in the antebellum era raised not only cotton but also wheat, hay, corn, oats, barley, and cattle and sheep but largely hogs for pork. The Lovelace place would have been no different."

The Lovelaces' eventual transformation from farmer-tanner to planter status as implied in Muschel's 1955 letter is an object lesson in an argument Gillespie makes in *Free Labor in an Unfree World*: "the growth of a traditional staple-crop economy and the slave labor system in the South created unique opportunities for skilled free white men to accumulate capital, land and slaves" (2004, 3). Since descendants of upwardly mobile farmers and/or artisanal families may at times have unwittingly distanced themselves from their yeoman roots and the weaving it may have entailed, depicting themselves instead as a formerly large slaveholding plantation family, our interests were further piqued when Johnson suggested that "unless someone had documentation, I'd go with the greater likelihood of it [the Lovelace coverlet] being produced at Troup Factory."

He further suggested that "the 'story' of slave-made would have perhaps started as a theory and developed into fact from people who did not know we had a factory here that did this sort of work." Johnson offered two scenarios in which, as an expert in the history of Troup County, he thought this coverlet might have been woven. "If you have cotton fabric that came from the family of James and Sara Jane Embry Lovelace, chances are it was manufactured at Troup Factory, also in Troup County, Ga. not more than a couple of miles southeast from where the Lovelace family lived. Troup Factory was our county's first cotton factory and made cloth of many descriptions from 1848 until about 1899 when it closed." Conversely, Johnson suggested that "if your textile is woolen, then it was most likely manufactured at Robertson Woolen Mill which was our county's first textile concern, started in 1847 and operated until after the War Between the States, and was located a couple of miles south of where the Lovelace family lived. However, if it is wool, it is also possible that the wool was taken to Robertson's Mill to be carded and rolled and that the cloth was manufactured at home. Both scenarios are possible with wool in Troup County during the antebellum era."[5]

Our correspondence with Johnson stoked our curiosity about Troup Factory and whether coverlets were really woven there.[6] And if they were, the questions arose of who was buying them, and where. In all of our visits to house museums and collections, we never once came across overshot identified as factory produced.

Additional Troup County histories cleared up this mystery.

Assessing the Lovelace coverlet in a photograph we provided, Johnson noted that "all those precise and differing sized squares . . . hand done loom work is seldom this neat and perfect with the lines, as machine run looms would be getting each pass of the shuttle equally tight as the previous." However, counting threads on the actual fragment at the Cooper Hewitt some time later, we saw a number of weaving faults that point to its hand-produced status, for example, the variation of twist of the woolen yarn as well as counting mistakes in ground weft. A close count of supplemental weft (wool yarn) of the original showed errors in pick insertions, another convincing sign of hand production. Further, Troup Factory records indicate that the Brooks family, who had founded the factory, possessed a large number of coverlets. According to factory historian William H. Davidson, these coverlets were not produced at the factory (though the yarn was probably spun and dyed there), but they were used as "toll" (payment) for milled goods (1971, 316).

While it became increasingly clear that this coverlet was not produced in the factory, Clark Johnson was not too far off the mark with his comment that "its general appearance is just too much like one we know was done at Troup Factory in the 1850s." This coverlet could have been traded there.

While the Lovelace fragment appears in association with slaves, to understand how and why the Lovelace and other geometric overshot designs are boundary objects that return in the world of modern twentieth- and twenty-first-century art by makers like Laurie Herrick and Christy Matson, as well as in such venerable cultural institutions as San Francisco's De Young Museum, both slave and high art contexts must be situated against a regional history in which coverlets were created and valued by a politicized yeoman community. We have explored how visual and academic histories of the region have been marred by post–Civil War ideologies depicting the antebellum southern landscape as devoid of yeoman and their handcrafts. But to really ascertain how and why yeoman coverlets became overshot with political concerns, we need to examine the very materiality of these forms.

Geometric Overshot Coverlets

A coverlet dated to 1773 from New York is the earliest documented overshot fabric in the United States, though the term appears in probate inventories a bit earlier (Ulrich 2001, 292–93). Historic records of Georgia phonetically spell the word as *coverlet, coverlid, coverlit, kivverlet,* and so forth. During the eighteenth and nineteenth centuries, domestically manufactured coverlets were woven from handwritten patterns called drafts (or draughts) that had been handed down as treasured heirlooms (still held in special-collections libraries and museums).

These drafts can contain clues about where patterns or weavers came from or who devised them. Some settlers had brought patterns with them to the new world; similar to other craft practices, overshot weaving has its origins around the world with variations in materials and loom styles that depended on climate and geographic environment.

Working on a four-harness counterbalance loom, nineteenth-century coverlet weavers typically used wool for the pattern and cotton (as opposed to their eighteenth-century counterparts' reliance on linen) for the ground.[7] The wool—from a farmer's own sheep or acquired through local trade networks—was often cleaned, carded, and spun on the farm. The production of cotton yarn had a more complicated trajectory, especially after the invention of spinning jennies (1770) and the cotton gin (1794), but for planter residences away from the coast prior to the arrival of rail in the 1820s, cleaning, carding, and spinning cotton was usually done on the farm.

In her *Country Life in Georgia in the Days of My Youth (Lived 1835–1930)*, Rebecca Felton (1919, 30) writes that on her grandmother's plantation "there were no such things as 'comforts' eighty years ago, but quilt making was never interrupted, winter or summer, and in early Georgia homes woolen 'coverlids' woven at home, and quilts innumerable, made by hand, were the bed coverings in all such well-to-do Georgia homes." Felton also describes the production of pre–cotton gin cloth:

> When my grandmother, Lucy Swift, began housekeeping, wool and flax were the dependence of housekeepers for clothing their families. Silk culture was exploited in Gen. Oglethorpe's time, but the use of cotton was handicapped. Before there were any cotton gins, the cotton lint was picked from the seed by human fingers. The lint was then carded by hand, spun on homemade wheels, then reeled into what were called "hanks," by use of home-made reels, then the warp was prepared for the home-made loom, by a variety of processes, all tedious and slow and all the work done by the house mother and her helpers. The thread was "sized" with a thin corn meal mush, then rolled on to home-made corn-cob spools from these stiffened "hanks," then the spools were carefully placed and manipulated on warping bars, then rolled on the beam of the loom, then drawn thread by thread into the "harness," keeping exact count of each thread, one to go up and another to go down when the treadles were moved by the weaver's foot, then carefully pulled through what was called a "sley," fashioned from canes gathered in swamps. After all this was performed the soft spun thread for "filling" was carefully transferred to small spools that were fitted into "shuttles." The warp being thus made ready for the weaver's shuttle, the process of cloth making was nearly accomplished, so the weaver pressed one treadle with her right foot and rushed the shuttle through, then pressing the other treadle with her other foot, she again dashed the shuttle back again, each time beating up the "filling" by fierce muscular strength in her arms. In this slow, tedious, intricate and nerve-racking and painstaking way all the wearing apparel of the masses was constructed. (30–31)

Figure 18 Loom room off the kitchen in Historic Meadow Garden, home of George Walton, ca. 1792, Augusta, Georgia. Colonial properties are often exhibited with kitchen looms; this site was staged by the Georgia State Society of the Daughters of the American Revolution.

As imported machine cloth became increasingly affordable and available in the 1820s, planter women in Georgia turned their energies to perfecting what they considered to be fine handcrafts such as needlework and appliqué quilting.

The preference for these arts as well as the yarns, fabrics, and tools used to make them were enabled by shifts in larger production, trade, and distribution infrastructures (see Beckert 2015). Improvements in dye technologies also improved the optical parameters of the hand arts.

Prior to the availability of synthetic dyes in the second half of the nineteenth century, a variety of natural dyestuffs were used to color yarns. Black walnut was used to produce brown, madder root or cochineal for red, pokeweed for a pinkish purple, and indigo for blue. Blacks, greens, oranges, and deep purples were achieved using more than one dyestuff, but require multiple trips to a dyepot. Imported and found mordants from metals such as alum, iron, copper, and tin both set the dye and heightened the color. To prevent colors from fading, plant-based mordants, such as oak gall, pomegranate, and sorrel-sourced tannin helped make dye fast. As anyone who still works with natural dyes knows, coloring materials for weaving has always been and remains a time-consuming activity that requires tremendous skill and volumes of materials.

Brown, black, pinkish purple, and blue predominate in upcountry coverlets. This made sense insofar as walnut, pokeberry, and indigo were available to yeoman. Samples containing vibrant red, possibly dyed with locally grown madder root (an early colonial export crop) are rare. And recipes for making bright scarlet red dye that call for madder root were complicated. The other alternative to creating brilliant fiery red yarn was the easy-to-use but expensive cochineal, imported from Central America and Mexico (see plate 5).

Of the commonly used dyestuff, tannin-rich walnut is one of the few locally sourced natural materials that does not depend on a mordant. Adding iron deepens the dark brown toward black, a color popular during the Victorian era. Iron additions might account for fiber degradation in brownish-black nineteenth-century coverlets, as the iron degrades the wool over time. Overdying with indigo was another way to create a blacker shade of brown, but this also added time to the dyeing process.

Pokeberries yield pinkish-purple (mauve) shades in yarn. Contemporary light- and wash-fast pokeberry studies remind us that the color visible today in historic coverlets is not always the color that was intended or used. Colorfastness tests show that wool, soaked for ten or more days in a fermented pokeberry bath, creates a deep burgundy or brilliant scarlet, much like what results with cochineal, although after time in the light, the color fades to the kinds of brownish-pink shades frequently seen today.[8] And, of course, yeoman weavers may not have always had either the financial or geographic resources to acquire cochineal.

As a result of yet another surge in popularity within the contemporary craft revival, many contemporary readers are familiar with the impressive range of blue hues created using indigo. Indigo is by far the most popular color used in historic American decorative textiles, and while this was not the case in the specifically southern collections we visited, blue does appear frequently and is often accompanied by a narrative of "grown on the farm, dyed on the farm." A brief history of North American indigo production reveals why this is a compelling but spurious narrative.

Indigo, Rice, and Cotton

By the seventeenth century, indigo dye dominated global textile dye trade, and two of the most color rich varieties, *Indigofera tinctoria* (Asian) and *Indigofera suffruticosa* (Central and South American) were available for purchase throughout colonial America (see Feeser 2013). But dyeing with indigo is more complicated than with dyestuffs like walnut or pokeberry because indigotin, the main coloring agent found in indigo, is insoluble in water, thereby necessitating a chemical reduction to color fiber.

The various growing regions cultivate, harvest, and process the dyestuff in their own ways. The simplest variation is an ancient method: the fresh leaf vat is made and used immediately upon harvest, but the dye has reduced fastness and produces a less concentrated color (see plate 6).

The composting and fermentation technique is more forgiving. Here, fresh leaves are allowed to compost, then formed into a ball and dried for future use. This method has been widely used in France and Japan, as well as by West African Hausa and Yoruba dyers (Cardon 2007).

But when large-scale commercial production is required, dyers use the more complex process of extracting indigo paste. Developed in India, the Caribbean, and Central America, this multistep process results in small cakes that are highly concentrated but lightweight. These cakes are ideal for long-distance trade. Plantations around the world used this third method to create indigo dye.

In the decades leading up to the Revolutionary War, indigo plantations spread rapidly in coastal South Carolina (and more tenuously in Georgia), with a handful of entrepreneurial planters committed to joining the global trend (Pressly 2013). In 1740, Eliza Lucas Pinckney famously planted indigo from her family's plantation in Antigua on their South Carolina Wappoo Plantation (Feeser 2013).

After the Revolutionary War, three factors led to a collapse in U.S. indigo production: England stopped purchasing indigo from former colonies, the price of American indigo fell, and competition increased from warmer producing regions. And though some continued to produce indigo, most planters turned their energies toward more lucrative market crops, such as rice and sea-island cotton. Additionally, the process of extracting commercially viable dye was described as a noxious, laborious, and "unhealthy" task in a 1848 report by the Agricultural Association of the State of Georgia in a discussion of why indigo was disappearing as an export crop in the South Carolina (Meyers 2008, 95). And of course, the Georgia agricultural board was looking to both policy and practice in South Carolina, since economic, social, and political interests as well as land typology cut across the border between the two states.

Genealogical records show that planter families in South Carolina and Georgia were also crossing that border. The legend presented to tourists at popular sites like the Drayton Plantation (founded by a member of the Drayton family of the Magnolia Plantation) has South Carolina, a colony of wealthy Englishman with economic ties to Caribbean plantation holdings, as the envied sibling to the younger (and less wealthy) Georgia, a philanthropic experiment of small farms and villages with strict laws prohibiting slavery. Finding themselves on the losing end of a competition for market shares against South Carolinians who were increasing their wealth with profitable cash crops (mainly rice and indigo) reliant on slave labor, Georgian settlers began to demand the rights to own not just larger tracts of land but also slaves. By 1751, the official ban on slavery was lifted in Georgia, and the story of Tara, the South as an agrarian planter-slave society eventually given its most powerful visual expression in films like *Gone with the Wind*, found its beginnings (see plate 7).

Prior to the Revolutionary War, low-country planters used slaves for the cultivation of rice, indigo, and long-staple cotton. The use of slavery plus the invention of the cotton engine, or gin, in 1793 made growing short-staple cotton in the upland regions more economical. As Rebecca Felton described it, before Eli Whitney's gin, separating the seeds from the fluff was extremely time consuming.

By another account it would have taken a field hand a full eighteen months to remove all of the seeds from a single bale of cotton (Lacques 2006). Since the cotton gin accelerated the deseeding process by a factor of fifty and decreased the number of slaves required to work each acre of cotton, planters began growing more short-staple cotton, and along with yeoman farmers, expanded settlement areas westward on cotton-producing lands. Short-staple cotton soon emerged as a primary cash crop (see plate 8).

In 1793 the South produced about ten thousand bales of cotton. By 1835, southern farmers grew a million bales, and by midcentury, cotton constituted two-thirds of U.S. exports (much of which went to British textile mills). As the cotton industry expanded, so did the South's use of household textiles. But not everyone in Georgia grew cotton as a cash crop. Today, despite eighty years of research to the contrary, the image of a landscape dominated by cotton planters and their slaves persists, with little consideration for yeoman weavers and their families.

The Yeoman

Socially, politically, economically, and even visually, the antebellum southern landscape was far more diverse than the picture advanced by Hollywood movies. Vlach (2004) notes that the architecture of each southern region was as distinct as the various crops and planting styles entailed by geographical differences. And not all planters lived in mansions with column-lined porticos.

In fact, according to John Forsyth's 1851 address to the Alabama Horticultural Society, southern planters lived in cabins of roughhewn wood. This was echoed by Olmsted in *The Cotton Kingdom* (1861) with his description of a Louisiana plantation as a log cabin, with an open shed and piazza in front, only one door, and no glass in the windows (103). But popular neoclassical architecture styles begin to penetrate the southern landscape in the mid-nineteenth century; as yeoman planters gained wealth, they would add columns or a porch to existing structures to mimic classical Greek architectural styles (102).

In the case of the Callaway Plantation (Wilkes County, Ga.), in 1860 the yeoman family demonstrated their increased wealth by starting construction on a Greek Revival plantation-style home (it wasn't completed until after the Civil War). We found no additional evidence to confirm this, but docents in 2012 explained that the classical brick mansion, with its two-story column-lined portico, served as the model for Margaret Mitchell's iconic Tara in her 1936 novel, *Gone with the Wind* (fig. 19).[9] During the following decades, as the Tara vision gained ground as an authentic view of the plantation South, the subsistence-farming yeomanry were simultaneously demoted to bumpkin status across multiple discursive forums, both popular and academic (Escott 1985; Van-Tassel 2002).

But the real antebellum yeomanry, who had been viewed by planters as representing a potential threat to their own privilege, had developed a distinct proclivity as "plain style people, living in plain style houses, equipped with plain style furniture" as emblematic of their unique cultural, economic, and political identity, in contrast to the style of wealthy planters (Atlanta History Center 2006, 7). Today, piedmont plain-style house museums across Georgia routinely display a rich array of plain-style material culture, including looms, drafts, spinning wheels, and, of course, overshot geometric coverlets that were woven and treasured by the white yeoman during the first half of the nineteenth century.

The original Callaway log cabin (built in 1785) and the federal plain-style residence (built in 1790 and occupied until 1869) are examples of this yeomanesque style. Today, these buildings are staged to represent the property during the colonial period (the period from 1790 to 1864 is not represented on this site). Both display coverlets on the beds.

In the plain-style house, a spinning wheel and loom occupy a corner in the main bedroom (fig. 20). With the Callaway family's "economic situation improv[ing], they abandoned their log cabin for a more spacious home, the Federal Plainstyle house, and then used the cabin as a kitchen. This two-story, four room plainstyle house contains furnishings typical of the 1790's including a loom."[10]

So, while the economic dominance of a planter class is clearly expressed in financial documents, other records indicate the existence of a complex, pluralistic system in which the yeoman constituted a large

Figure 19 Greek Revival–style portico at the Callaway Plantation (1869), Wilkes County, Georgia.

Figure 20 Loom in an upstairs bedroom in the federal plain-style home (1790–1869) at Callaway Plantation. Now furnished in colonial style, this remained the family residence until after the Civil War.

portion of the population and had a significant impact on political, economic, and cultural realities and a demonstrated sense of class consciousness (McCurry 1995; Owsley 1949). By drawing on a wide variety of sources—including church records, wills, estate records, county-court minutes, trial records, mortgage books, deed books, tax books, memoirs, and newspaper accounts—Frank Owsley recast the lives of the yeomanry in his *Plain Folk of the Old South*. He (1949, 8) argued, against many popular accounts, that "the core of the social structure was a massive body of plain folk who were neither rich nor very poor. These were employed in numerous occupations; but the majority secured their food, clothing, and shelter from some rural pursuit, chiefly farming and livestock grazing."

Prior to the Civil War, these yeomen farmers were wary of market capitalism and therefore "fundamentally committed to producing for household consumption and local exchange" (Hahn 2006, 89). Hahn's *Roots of Southern Populism* (2006) covers not just yeoman of the upcountry, but also those living in the pine barrens, alpine, hill, and black-belt regions. These were independent, self-reliant, subsistence farmers who practiced "safety-first" agriculture.

Such a strategy ensured that they could meet all of their own needs. What they could not grow or make with their own hands, they would trade with neighbors, merchants, or nearby artisans. A "safety-first" approach inured them from some of the booms and busts of larger market economies during the first half of the nineteenth century.

Yeomen occupied all five Georgia regions and, as already noted, are characterized by ownership of 200 or fewer improved acres with few or no slaves. This land ownership threshold privileges planter-style agriculture while overlooking the significant economic value of unimproved land to the raising of livestock (see Kersey 2012). But when we consider the conditions that encourage coverlet weaving, we should consider the availability of wool. The wool yield according in the 1850 Agriculture Census was moderate to high (7,000–18,000 lb.) in counties where women wove coverlets during the antebellum period. The 1850 census data tracking the value of home manufacture suggest that regions with high percentages of white residents to black residents and greater amounts of unimproved to improved acreage (yeoman farms) met or exceeded the norm.

Of course, the larger economic context of yeoman life was the burgeoning cotton industry: as the profitable, slave labor–driven cotton industry was expanding and the planter class was accumulating capital in the form of land, slaves, machinery, and imported material goods, the yeomanry were being pushed farther and farther inland, farming for subsistence and cash, and increasingly disempowered through planter-backed legislation.[11]

But after the late 1840s, as the cotton economy rebounded from a slump and railroads and the cotton as a cash crop continued to push the frontier westward, more and more yeoman were drawn, albeit reluctantly, into the vortex of the cotton economy, specializing in cotton but at the expense of their own self-sufficiency (Ford 1988, 18–19). The physical devastation wrought by cotton on arable land left many with rising debts that in turn supported a market favorable to cotton over corn and other foodstuffs. Many yeoman abandoned the diversified planting practices that had once shielded them from the vagaries of the market. This loss was, however, somewhat mitigated by the availability of new goods that came with railroad lines.

Coverlets as Political Objects

Much of textile-based material culture (e.g., clothing) was produced in the household by plantation women with help from owned or leased enslaved labor. An exception was weaving, which seems to have been increasingly relegated to outbuildings like loom houses and barns, antebellum spaces supposedly largely devoid of white women's labor, at least in the Lost Cause narrative of the southern plantation lady. In reality, white planter women made substantial contributions to household labor. Edith Rose, a descendant of the Spring Hill Plantation family outside of Rome, Georgia, donated coverlets and quilts to the Atlanta History Center in 1995. She also provided a document conveying her thoughts on the misrepresentation of the labor of white southern plantation women:

> Generally speaking, it seems the majority of people seem to think slaves did all the hard, tedious work in the South in the more affluent homes. This is not true in our family and there are historians who agree. . . . But slaves or no slaves, the women of the families did the actual weaving of every coverlet in this collection. . . . Despite legends, moonlight, mockingbirds and

> magnolia, Southern women held very closely to the weaving and quilting rooms because of their own extensive families . . . 11 and 12 children commonplace. That called for a great quantity of covers (*kivers* in the mountain country) for the many beds, company galore which called for more beds and each house in the slave quarters has to have covers for their beds. And all those hordes—with the exception of guests—had to have covers for their backs. They wove sheets, blankets, cotton goods for underclothing and outer summer dresses, table linen. . . . Southern women ran small factories . . . those giddy belles that we read so much baloney about!!! (and still these charming men of ours want to keep on "protecting" us . . .).[12]

Of course, Rose's letter reflects problems with gendered (and racialized) representations of labor and the meanings of labor, the long histories of which reach right into the present.

By the end of the 1820s, with the arrival of the Jacquard attachment and subsequent popularity of the "figured" and "fancy" patterns, women in the Midwest, the Mid-Atlantic, and New England (but not in the South) began to commission coverlets from professional male weavers (Peck 1990). These coverlets and their weavers are featured as decorative Americana in private collections and highlighted in *Coverlets and the Spirit of America: The Shein Coverlets* (2002) by Melinda Zonger, *American Coverlets and Their Weavers: Coverlets from the Collection of Foster and Muriel McCarl* (2002) by Clarita S. Anderson, and other books. These texts contain photographs of coverlets and a bibliography of known weavers. Meanwhile, the value-giving qualities of the domestically woven, amateur coverlet with a southern provenance remain relatively unknown in these circles, perhaps because they were made and invested with meaning by a relatively obscure group: yeoman women.

In fact, while historical estate records note both the economic value and the high quality of home-woven coverlets, they are often discussed in terms of their heirloom qualities, a connection to domesticity, or the making of a comfortable home for one's family rather than their place in the household economy (see Bress 2003). Some have even doubted that these textiles were made at home, as in Patricia J. Keller's review of Locklair's *Quilts, Coverlets, and Counterpanes: Bedcoverings from the Museum of Early Southern Decorative Arts and Old Salem Collections*: "was there really a cast of 'home' weavers whose work can be visually distinguished from that of the 'professional's' as Locklair implies? Or was weaving typically practiced in or near the household by skilled artisans for both family needs and market consumption?" (Keller 1988, 102).

Another degrading perspective on southern overshot is exemplified in a 1922 edition of the *Bulletin of the Pennsylvania Museum* that describes a newly acquired set of linen (or more likely cotton) and wool woven coverlets dated between 1750 and 1850 from Tennessee, Kentucky, and Georgia reported to represent the development of "a rudimentary art." The museum report describes how the preponderance of blue dye must have lent a touch of color to a "dun and arduous existence" ("Hand-Woven Coverlets" 1922). Instead of celebrating a sophisticated art form undertaken by choice with pride and creative virtuosity, the bulletin portrays a make-do people barely eking out an existence.

Given that the Pennsylvania museum acquired the coverlets made in Tennessee in the years after the Civil War and that they are dated 1750–1850, it is possible they were woven on southern plantations by planter women with the help of, or entirely by, slaves (which would cut against the hegemonic version of women that became the fictional Scarlet O'Hara and Melanie Hamilton Wilkes who lived anything but a dun and arduous existence). But it is just as likely, if not more so, that they were woven by yeoman women. In some ways, coverlet weaving worked as an embodiment of a political commitment by the yeoman partly precisely because it is a challenging, skilled art form rather than a crude, make-do folk practice.

In predominantly yeoman regions, it was assumed that women would need to contribute to farmwork and home manufacture, and indeed such work was central to women's roles as valued members of family and community (Wetherington 2005). The veritable flood along rail lines of cheap, industrial cloth from northern American and European manufacturers, coinciding with the rise of regional spinning mills in the South, decreased the need for labor-intensive hand production of cloth, but women with weaving skills continued to work on decorative objects, like coverlets (Joseph, Hamby, and Long 2004). They did so because the role of textiles—woven coverlets in particular—was integral to both the production and performance of their identity, which was distinct from the identity of antebellum planters (see Eelman 2008, 38).

In the century before the Civil War, women wove "homespun" as a symbol of republican self-sufficiency, indexing an affinity with a Jeffersonian worldview (see plate 9 for contemporary interpretation of this idea). Advocates promoted traditional women's craft in agricultural journals (e.g., an 1843 edition of *Southern Cultivator* called on farmers to support womenfolk in industry and patriotism), in farmers' societies (where, in reaction to federally imposed tariffs on imported goods, such groups in South Carolina awarded prizes for locally woven coverlets and counterpanes), and in cottage industries (e.g., the short-lived S.C. Homespun Company offered locally produced cloth to patriotic Charlestonians from 1808 to 1815) (R. Griffin 1961).

Making textiles (and other plain-style goods) instead of importing them was not only a badge of economic autonomy and cultural belonging but an index of a political identity reflecting a commitment to self-sufficiency opposed to the conspicuous consumption of imported goods or the honing of accomplishments like needlework. Southern yeomen women demonstrated little interest in competing with planters in the fineries of bourgeois hobby work or consumerism. Instead, in prefiguring contemporary work by the artist Allison Smith, who critically engages how the performance and display of textiles have been implicated in the making of cultural values (particularly those related to nationalism), women yeomen weavers were in essence defining a style for a new nation.

Here we see a shifting kaleidoscope of factors—personal, political, and economic—contributing to the value of the yeoman coverlet. Like quilting or embroidery, weaving requires skill and time, but it is a rather solitary practice, so individual women or small household groups would have worked on them (alone or serially). The fact that women signed and bequeathed their weaving drafts is testament to this. Drafts kept among family documents were treasured artifacts of weaving work and evidence of a weaver's literacy. That they were preserved in family archives attests to their perceived value. For example, drafts are carefully preserved along with weaving accoutrements in the Fox-Genovese and Jewell family archives at the University of Georgia (Fox-Genovese 1988; fig. 21).[13]

The Jones family is said to have sequestered a coverlet among other valuables hidden from Yankee forces. Midway Museum papers suggest that when the Reverend Charles Colcock Jones from Liberty Country, Georgia, died during the Civil War, his widow, Mary, fled her "beloved home MonteVideo" for New Orleans.[14] She hid among her belongings her treasured heirlooms, one of which was the (misidentified as

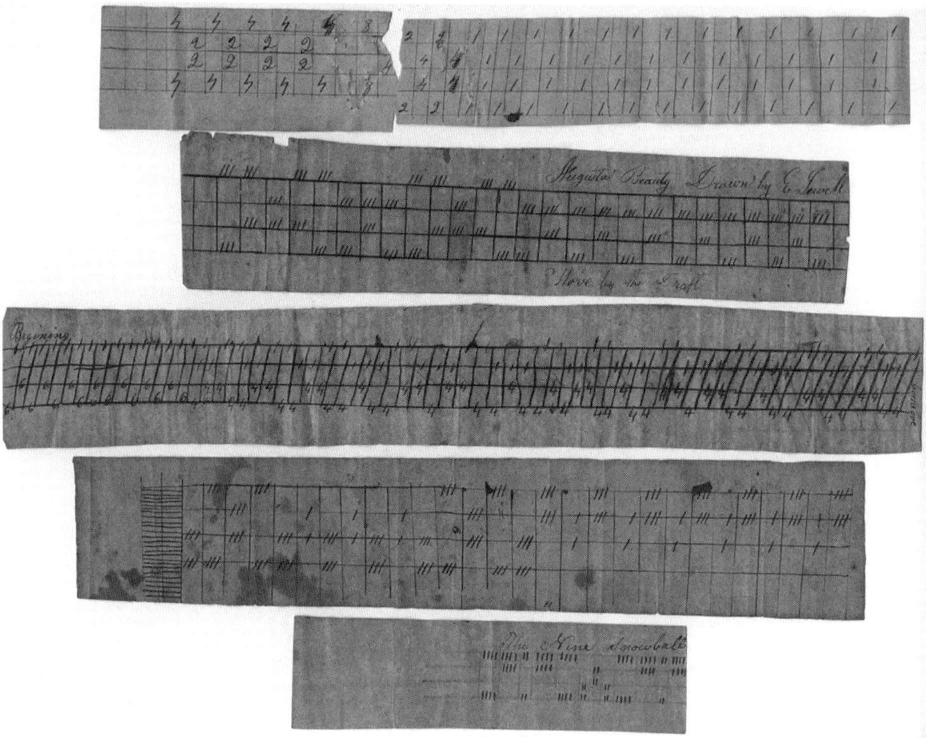

Figure 21 Weaving drafts found in the Jewell Family Collection (1809–1900). Courtesy of Hargrett Rare Book and Manuscript Library / University of Georgia Libraries.

Jacquard-woven) geometric overshot coverlet now housed at the Midway Museum.

These geometric overshot coverlets came to embody a more explicit political aesthetic when cheaper machine-produced cotton cloth and yarn freed the home loom from practical weaving places. In this context, skillfully handwoven heirloom showpieces cast into sharp relief the production, distribution, and consumption of factory-produced commodity cloth that was dependent on unskilled wage laborers, who in the northern states were the daughters and children of rural yeoman farmers (Marks 1996a).

Also in the North, early feminist and rural activists believed that productive domestic manufacture advanced the role of women as equals in the farm economy (Jensen 1988, 124). Agricultural societies and rural publications of the nineteenth century explicitly acknowledged the weaving as part of a greater political movement. This artpolitical energy is exemplified in the 1820 publication of *Dialogs of Domestic and Rural Economy and the Fashionable Follies of the World*, written by early feminist and controversial Hudson Valley Quaker, Hannah Barnard. The first writing by a woman on domestic economy focused entirely on rural woman, *Dialogs* extolled the virtues of learning productive skills such as how to spin, weave, knit, and sew, in opposition to what she regarded as frivolous refined hobby crafts, such as decorative embroidery.

Woman's household production was also encouraged by political figures and commentators in order to support the self-sufficiency and independence of small farms, and in the years preceding the Civil War, to support pro-slavery strategies to keep yeoman households out of debt through productive home industry. Woven mostly for household consumption, coverlets also entered into the marketplace with monetary value, appearing on the credit side of store ledgers and, though less easy to document, in trade (McCurry 1992). It is therefore not unreasonable to imagine the handwoven Lovelace fragment circulating as toll.

The substantial economic value of coverlets for both yeoman and planter alike is evidenced by the fact that they were listed in estate records, divorce decrees, and wills. For example, when John Lay of Gordon County died in 1862, inventory records indicate that a sell-off of his property included five coverlets sold at about $75 each. Adjusting for inflation, this would be about $1,330 in today's terms. Census records from

1860 show Lay as a yeoman, with ten slaves over the age of ten (and four slave children under the age of three).[15]

Likewise, a will devised by Joseph Pryor stipulated that at his death his wife would receive "one negro named Lucinda, one young sorrel mare . . . one saddle and bridle, two cows & calves two ewes of sheep, one bed & stead, all the quilts she has made whilst she has been living with me, one half the coverlids, also one half the counterpanes." Just in case the quantity was misinterpreted, the document reiterates: "it is understood that she only is to have one half of the coverlids & counterpains [white-on-white coverlets] she has made whilst living with me" (Pryor 1851).

Of course, the political economy driving class conflicts, women's identities, and the production and meaning of the overshot coverlet all change after the Civil War. The decades following that war were not kind to the independent small farmer when increasing staple crop agriculture, decreased landholdings, and market competition for commercial goods ushered in an era of industrial capitalism. The globalized capitalism we see today is the continuation of this trajectory.

The Authority of the Visual

Eighteenth- and nineteenth-century coverlet patterns represented the landscape or natural objects that would have been a part of weavers' everyday lives. The names of their patterns are instructive, for example pine trees, snowflakes, and orange peels. None of these appear to be political. But the patterns, or at least their names, sometimes referred to political events. The "Braddock's Defeat" pattern refers to a failed 1755 British military expedition (so, this name also suggests a historical legacy) while "Swepson and Littlefield" indexes a massive post–Civil War railroad embezzlement scandal that impacted many communities in North Carolina (Fenlon 1954; Miller and Schillo 2014).[16]

At a more formal level, however, the weaving structure generates a repeating geometric that works as an aesthetic manifestation of Jeffersonian republicanism in its rational, minimal, balanced symmetry and as a fractal system where each part operates independently but is a necessary part of the whole—in other words, it is a spectacular example of Jeffersonian political theory. It also indexes and foreshadows the emergence of the grid, especially as it relates to modernity and the increasing hegemony of pixelated modes of production, depiction, communication, and control. Both material and digital gridworks tame and translate time into space (and vice versa). And as we see in chapter 5, Anni Albers and other Bauhaus artists advanced the narrative of modernity and the grid that was taken up in contemporary work by artists, among them Laurie Herrick (with cotton remaining a central component over time since its by-products are now used by artists and designers in lenses, magnetic tapes, computer chip boards, flat-panel screens, digital imaging, and digital printing, and the like).

Framing this lineage is a challenge. Peter Dormer writes that, like Art (with a capital A), design—which is mainstream and represents dominant modes of production—is always an argument, while the power of craft, given its marginal status, is almost entirely rhetorical and symbolic (Dormer 1997). He further argues that craft represents counterculture, its production is already a form of dissent, and the choice of craft objects is always a self-conscious one (130). In the world of aesthetics, craft often strives toward the minor literature about which Gilles Deleuze and Félix Guattari (1968; and in 1983 with coauthor Brinkley) write: a minor literature is not the literature of a minor language but the literature a minority makes in a major language to pry open a space that is both political and collective.

Minor literatures, like the work of Franz Kafka, involve "the deterritorialization of language, the connection of the individual to a political immediacy, and the collective assemblage of enunciation. We might as well say that minor no longer designates specific literatures but the revolutionary conditions for every literature within the heart of what is called great (or established) literature" (Deleuze and Guattari 1968, 17–18).

As scholars have done with work by novelists such as Alice Walker (Nayer 2010), literary genres like comics (La Cour 2016), or even contemporary art (O'Sullivan 2009), using the framework of minor literature with regard to language, politics, and collectivity can help us think through how the practice of "writing" woven coverlets articulates with larger cultural practices and power structures.

A minor literature does not operate in parallel with a major literature but rather works from within it, drawing from the elements of that literature, but using them in a different way. Yeomen rearticulated hegemonic textile elements in both form and content, creating counter-hegemonic material culture by weaving the selfsame cotton and wool commodities that served as the basis of planter-class primary accumulation. Overshot weaving, especially after 1820, was intrinsically political given the availability of industrially produced alternatives. Here, engaging in overshot weaving when you don't have to—as women yeomen did—calls to attention an entire apparatus. The appearance of nineteenth-century overshot thus necessarily contains the entrails of planter ascendency resulting from cotton-powered globalization. At the same time, the practice was a communal enunciation of an unfinalized, evolving, and variously understood identity. Minor literature, thus, has a sharp critical potential, but one that is not always guaranteed or realized.

So, although the term didn't make it into mainstream vocabulary until the first decade of the 2000s, as in the publication of Betsy Greer's *Knitting for Good!* (2008), many nineteenth-century coverlet weavers were "craftivists" *avant la lettre*. By harnessing fibers and the power of visual culture, women yeomen embedded counter-hegemonic cultural and political values into a form of visible public culture that could be displayed, circulated, and discussed. Their work could not help but denote reigning economic, social, and political dynamics tied to the cotton industry, a globalizing world economy, and a shifting racialized class landscape. These textiles blurred the boundaries between art and living, while their materiality rendered them powerful, if not subversive, amulets that underwent a slow process of selective appropriation within revivalist movements, as objects in museum and textile collections, and as ur-material for white box art.

Chapter 4 Pioneer Sisters

A little-known resource—the Jackson Sisters Family Papers—at the Georgia Archives contains selected belongings from six sisters. The Jackson sisters lived in Jones County both before the Civil War and well into the twentieth century.[1] Although the Jackson homestead was located within the Plantation Belt (Jones County reported 66% black inhabitance in the 1850 Census), the family was one in a community of yeoman farmers marked by the Jeffersonian virtue of independent proprietorship supported by the cooperative efforts of family and neighbors (Reidy 1992). Local lore stated that the sisters wove coverlets in the Georgia piedmont area well after the Civil War, a noteworthy point for a number of reasons.

As suggested in the previous chapter, woven coverlets were produced and used by the white yeomanry, small landowning family farmers who owned few or no slaves.[2] Before the war, the role of textiles—woven coverlets in particular—was integral to the both the production and social performance of self-reliance that worked in contrast to the lifestyles of planters with their imported textiles and European fineries purchased with cash acquired through their success in a market economy. Yeomen's "safety-first" agricultural strategy focused on growing foodstuffs, the excess of which could be bartered for goods. Farmers added commercial cash crops like cotton only as time and space allowed.

This strategy changed dramatically following the war. The expansion of rail lines to isolated communities, coupled with the introduction of commercial fertilizer, access to markets, and increased acreage of improved land, all encouraged cotton cultivation.[3] New exploitive credit systems forced small farmers to rely on staple crop agriculture, challenging their independence and fueling the fires of southern populism (Hahn 2006, 152). The notable decrease between 1860 and 1910 in the head of sheep per acre of land curtailed the availability of material for homespun wool. Finally, the capacity for home manufacture, as indicated by the reduction of weaving implements (looms and spinning wheels) in estate records from the last decades of the nineteenth century, dropped dramatically (Ferleger and Metz 2014, 123). All of these factors impacted self-sufficiency in home goods, particularly textiles (see Hanh 2006, 186).

The Jackson Sisters Family Papers yields information on what representations of coverlet weaving as an aesthetic practice reveal about these larger economic, political, and cultural dynamics. A case study of the sisters, particularly how the Jacksons were depicted as makers of the early and mid-twentieth century, shows how yeomen's local, do-it-yourself material culture was folded into early twentieth-century political aesthetics.

The Jackson Sisters

As a sociopolitical orientation, U.S. republicanism, taken up by Jefferson's Democratic-Republican Party (founded in 1791), supported the broad distribution of wealth, maintained a healthy suspicion of urban commercial interests, and was antiaristocratic. Early adherents were committed to individualism and sympathetic to European political movements advancing the rights of men, particularly the French Revolution, which was rooted in a Rousseauian celebration of human rights, freedom, egalitarianism, and hope for a better future.[4] But though Jefferson's party faded away after the 1820s, many of the ideals of the party lived on in field and cabin, particularly those related to the celebration of agrarian economies, plain folk, local control, and small independent farming families.

The story of the Jackson sisters is instructive in this regard, especially since the popular press drew rather nostalgically on these ideals to depict the sisters via their supposed weaving talents. A renewed interest in coverlets, like those associated with the Jacksons, was spurred by a nationalist movement that situated U.S. folk craft as a symbol of democracy, egalitarianism, and (more specifically to the South) "located the most unadulterated kernel of Americanness in the Anglo-Saxon traditions of Appalachia" (Jentleson 2013; Becker 1998). Similar to the nineteenth century, when many women could have acquired machine-made cloth, twentieth-century women bought or produced handcrafted items for the purposes of effecting a DIY aesthetic. This revival was a twentieth-century iteration of an even earlier revival (1820–60). The textiles in both cases, mid-nineteenth and early twentieth centuries, have a sign value, or meaning, that went well beyond their use value, or function, as bed coverings. In other words, they were political-aesthetic objects.

The Jackson sisters lived on a family farm of 300 acres near Hillsboro, Georgia, from 1847 to 1940. They remain local legends to those advancing the mission of the Jasper County Historical Foundation.[5] Although

Birth and death dates for the Jackson sisters and their mother

Margia A. Jackson (mother)	born February 27, 1822	died July 20, 1871
Julia Jackson	March 25, 1847	February 20, 1932
Mary (Betty) Jackson	January 2, 1849	February 16, 1935
Lucy Ann Jackson	November 2, 1852	December 4, 1933
Margia C. Jackson	April 6, 1857	January 9, 1934
Sarah A. Jackson	August 23, 1859	November 25, 1916
Cynthia Jackson	April 21, 1861	March 19, 1940

SOURCE: "Information about the Jackson Sisters," RootsWeb, http://www.rootsweb.ancestry.com/~gajasper/infoabtjackson.htm.

the farm falls within the Plantation (Black) Belt, the labor and homestead's acreage listed on the census indicate that this was yeoman property. Estate records are unclear as to whether or not Lewis Jackson, the father, owned slaves, but it is likely that he owned a few, since "the Lower Piedmont region had more slave holders than farms, which mean that practically every farmer there, as well as some town people, owned one or more slaves" (Harper 1922, 19). Although in the Upper Piedmont region the vast majority of farms were owned by yeomen, in the Lower Piedmont the Jacksons and other small farming families settled among plantations, an important aesthetic and social differentiation made by students of the nineteenth-century southern landscape (see McCurry 1992; Kersey 2009; Ferleger and Metz 2014).

The family patriarch, Lewis Jackson, was born in 1820 in Georgia. His wife, Margery (Margie) Ann Carmichael Jackson, was born in Georgia in 1824.[6] The couple had six daughters: Julia, Mary (Betty), Lucy Ann, Margia (Marge), Sarah, and Cynthia (fig. 22). A son was born on July 6, 1863, but died after only two weeks.

Lewis Jackson served in Company D in the Sixty-Sixth Regiment of the Georgia Volunteer Infantry and died during the Civil War (Slay 2001, 14). The 1850, 1880, and 1900 census records list one additional family member residing on the family property: Lewis's older brother, Andrew Jackson (born 1817). Andrew's occupation is listed as farm labor. Though the family homestead is gone, records show that the Jackson sisters, their mother, and a baby brother are buried there, many in unmarked graves.

They were hard-working and long-lived (with the three eldest living into their eighties), but none of the sisters married or had children. Sarah, the only Jackson daughter ever to have been engaged, was killed

Figure 22 The six Jackson sisters, Jones County, 1880s. Top row, left to right: Julia, Cynthia, Sallie. Bottom row: Mary ("Bettie" or "Betty"), Lucy, Margie. Charcoal drawing courtesy of the Georgia Archives, Vanishing Georgia Collection, jon081.

at the age of forty-seven when a tree fell on her in 1916. Cynthia Jackson, the youngest sister, outlived the others, dying in 1940 at the age of seventy-eight. At that time, the Jackson sisters' estate was bequeathed by Cynthia to Rufus Garland, a neighbor who had helped the sisters from time to time. Also unmarried with no heirs, Garland later gave what was left of the collection to his own sister, a Mrs. G. A. Wynnes, who in turn left it to her granddaughters. By 1978, the collection from the Jackson sisters' homestead had been donated to the Georgia Archives in Morrow (Pederson 1978, 95).

Figure 23 Detail of woven coverlet. Courtesy Jackson Sisters Family Papers, acc. 1970-0297M, Georgia Archives.

The Jackson Sisters Family Papers is an outstanding compilation of artifacts documenting yeoman life. It consists of 466 items dated roughly between 1847 and 1935. It is well kept and in good shape. The collection contains hundreds of letters to the sisters, several newspaper articles, medical remedies, photo albums, socks, receipts, bibles, dressmakers' pattern, weaving drafts, a white coverlet, a patterned overshot coverlet (fig. 23), and other items. There was no documentation attached to any of the textiles, so it is unclear who made them, where, or when.

As of May 2019, none of the objects in the collection had been digitized. The archivist noted that very few people had ever looked at the collection.[7] The apparent lack of interest in the Jackson sisters archive fits cleanly into the general lack of research on the Georgian yeomanry in general as compared to the preponderance of research concerning planters and enslaved Africans. We are not aware of any aspect of this collection having been involved in published research or as part of an exhibit, for example, on early twentieth-century farming or colonial revivalism, although the story of these sisters would certainly make for a compelling show.

From the Archive

Among the documents was a 1929 newspaper article by Susan Myrick, an editor of the Georgia Magazine section of the *Macon Telegraph*. Her "Five Sisters Lead Pioneer Lives" appeared as a full page offering in the Sunday Lifestyle section.

Born in 1893, Myrick is well-known for her role as an advisor for matters pertaining to southern culture for the film adaptation of Margaret Mitchell's *Gone with the Wind*, but she had a long and varied career as a journalist. Myrick's life and work can be viewed in the light of her commitments to both feminism and rural activism. The "Five Sisters" piece (fig. 24), in presenting the Jackson sisters as remarkable, independent women representing country life, reflects her interest in both.[8]

Myrick celebrates the sisters as throwbacks to a revered but vanishing past. To set the scene for readers, she opens the article with a claim that "this is the day of equal rights" before describing how the sisters eke out a somewhat "meager and pathetic" existence in a farmhouse at the end of a dirt road.

Using dialect and poetic depiction as literary devices, Myrick tells of how she became lost en route to the house but reports that "a group of

Figure 24 The lead for Susan Myrick's first article on the Jackson sisters, in the Sunday, May 6, 1929, Lifestyle section of the *Macon Telegraph*. Image courtesy of the *Macon Telegraph*.

Negroes digging a grave in a lonely country churchyard" were able to give her directions. This approach to journalism is not only descriptive and evocative of a disappearing way of life, but it signals to readers that Myrick was traveling some distance—physically, linguistically, and socially—to enter into a territory not just unfamiliar to her but possibly also exotic. This entry narrative establishes the authority of the writer as an eyewitness, as having been in a place that you, the reader, has not.

Once she establishes her own presence in the situation and thus her right to report, Myrick portrays the Jackson sisters' world. In an Olmsted-like fashion, she writes that their rugless floors are scoured to white, the rails on rocking chairs have been torn off by age and use, and the sitting room is poorly lit by a single sashless window with no glass. Writing in dialect to report what the Jackson sisters say also depicts them as rough-hewn country folk. This strategy makes the standard English that Myrick reserves for herself seem by comparison to be smooth, urban, and sophisticated. But when she turns her eye to material culture, the dilapidated condition of the house recedes in contrast to her attitude toward the "beautiful furnitures of a generation agone," such as a spool bed with a coverlid of such "hand-woven beauty that it made me gasp."

When queried, the sisters admit to having "spun" the coverlet. Shunning technological advances and the increasing availability of machine-made threads and textiles, "Miss Betsey" tells Myrick: "'Course, I dyed that thread' . . . with a voice full of scorn for all who would buy thread already dyed" (Myrick 1929, 6). (It is a curiosity that Myrick called her Miss Betsey rather than Betty—at times spelled Bettie—as other sources indicate Mary was called).

Despite Myrick's politely repeated pleas to see their loom, the sisters refused and scolded her with what she describes as withering contempt. "You wouldn't know nuthin bout it ef I wuz to show hit to you," Betty/Betsey said. "You ain't seed much. An I ain't a going to git hit fer ya. Nor they shaint git it" (6). The article never clarifies whether the sisters possess a loom or not; in the article, Betty/Betsey certainly allows Myrick to believe that they have a loom, but diverts the interview away from looms and "coverlids" to discuss a quilt pattern, post war scarcity, and farming.

In asserting poverty as a heritage, ethic, and value, Betty/Betsey asserts the value of self-reliance (a value consistent with Jeffersonian ideals of democracy interpreted by the antebellum yeoman class). The back and forth between Myrick and the sisters is delivered with something of a wink and a nod to readers, who Myrick surely would have expected to be educated and worldly enough to assign a kind of authentic purity to these Luddite makers of handmade crafts (as did she).

The nostalgic "Pioneer" text in the *Macon Telegraph* is supported by a large, above-the-fold collage of photos. Recalling the spinning of cotton or wool, the collage consists of five images arranged in a wheel-and-spoke design. Photos of four sisters are arranged around a center photograph of the fifth sister (Sarah was already deceased) standing beside a spinning wheel, an interesting choice given that the sisters explicitly declare that they had at some unspecified time in the past given up spinning and weaving in order to run the farm.

Myrick's text and photos were consistent with the portrayal of traditional, authentic makers unsullied by the trappings of modernity. Some of the other images in the Jackson sisters collection, for example an undated photo of the two sisters posing with a wheel in front of a coverlet (fig. 25) and another of Betty blowing a horn, show the sisters in a similar light. This depiction of the nostalgic yeoman persists in published work on the sisters with remarkable consistency. For example, Carol Krom (2003b, 3) writes that "the eldest sister, Julia, acted as farm manager, while Bettie [Betty] was in charge of cooking over the open hearth, gardening, and the chickens. In the growing season, all but Bettie worked in the fields, plowing with a mule, plating hoeing and harvesting. Bettie called them to the table by blowing an ancient horn."

Spinning Stories

Despite all of the complexities involved in untangling fact from fiction about southern antebellum material culture, it is reasonable to assume that, by the 1840s, more textiles were produced industrially or imported than were produced on farms. In the case of plantation households, historical records support this assumption. In her study of North Carolina, Laurel Wilson (1986) argues that weaving was already on the wane during the nineteenth century and may have disappeared altogether had it not been for a resurgence of weaving in response to Civil War shortages. Just how much domestic spinning and weaving actually occurred in Georgia just before or during the Civil War is unclear.

Scholars agree that plantation and yeoman households spun and wove cloth for personal use and regional sale, but families were also purchasing commercially produced goods from regional, northern, and European mills. In the South, the Civil War leveled the material playing field between yeoman and planter-class families, or so the story goes. In this version of events, oft repeated in house and plantation museums, looms were dusted off and everyone—planter, slave, and yeoman alike—were back to spinning and weaving to meet their textile needs.

In northern cities, looms and spinning wheels were also dusted off, not out of necessity, but as staged events to support war efforts. This took place, for example, in popular New England Kitchen sections of aid fairs. These performances were meant to raise support and funds for the United State Sanitary Commission (predecessor to the Red Cross). These attractions focused on re-creating farmhouse life and, as described in a 1864 circular, to "reproduce the manners, customs, dress and if possible, the idiom of the time; in short, to illustrate the domestic life and habits of the people, to whose determined courage, sustained by their faith in God, we owe that government, so dear to every loyal heart" (quoted in Commission 1864, 73). Weaving and spinning thus became tied up with national pride.

Immediately after the Civil War, with the exception of a few regional pockets, spinning and weaving—as practices or as theater—seem to have all but disappeared. But myths are persistent, and so too was the power of the spinning wheel as image. The trope was enthusiastically reproduced across various media. For example, in *Spinning Stories* (1884) published as the post–Civil War craft revival was beginning, Louisa May Alcott (1832–1888) presents the spinning wheel as a time machine. Here, a grandmother teaches a group of children how to "spin" in stories tinged with morals and a heavy dose of historical romanticism. The spinning wheel as a rich symbol of textile production is used to take listeners back to better times.

The use of a spinning wheel to signal independence movements and an attachment to an imagined American past would have been familiar to early twentieth-century U.S. audiences. Beverly Gordon speaks specifically to the practice of needlework, but her claim that "by the 1920's, colonial revival needlework, represent[ed] a nationwide, populist, democratic form of expression, very much in keeping with the modernist

Figure 25 The Jackson sisters with spinning wheel. Postcard from the public domain.

agenda" (1998, 165) can be applied not only to handmade textiles but to crafts as a whole. The image of a woman with a spinning wheel was, then, a powerful icon, and handmade textiles "represent[ed] the old fashioned or the 'coziness' of days gone by," a more simple and noble American past understood against a new era "teeming with cities, radio broadcasts, and cars pouring off assembly lines" (164). This was not the first time that domestic textile production, particularly spinning and weaving, was used to evoke an imagined "better time," an era before the anxieties many people associated with globalized modernity took hold. And it would not be the last (see chapter 6).

A noteworthy midcentury example of the spinning wheel as political aesthetic comes to us in the form of an iconic photograph of Mahatma Gandhi. While Margaret Bourke-White's famous image of Gandhi with his cherished spinning wheel was not taken until 1946 for a *Life* magazine article (the year before Indian independence), the khadi (handspun and woven cloth) movement began in 1918 when Gandhi established a relief program for rural poor. In the thirty years between its inception and the photograph, Gandhi's support of khadi elevated the production of homespun material from a pragmatic practice to an ideological framework for India's nonviolent independence movement: if all Indians spun, wove, and wore Khadi, they would be free from dependence on foreign imports and on the road to self-governance. In 1948, Bourke-White's image captured the imagination of the American public when it was given center stage following Gandhi's assassination under the heading, "India Loses Her 'Great Soul'" (Cosgrove 2014).

Photographs of Gandhi (like Bourke-White's) and the association of spinning with soul and nation reverberated so strongly for *Life* readers because spinning for independence was already a familiar narrative to the U.S. public. Of course, it is important to note the great irony in drawing a relationship between images of Gandhi's support of handspun cloth as a vehicle of independence and America's romantic vision of its preindustrial origins was that Gandhi had first encouraged the revival of Indian handweaving traditions at a time when milled cloth imported from Europe and the United States had decimated Indian hand production.

Indian white cotton goods, before the establishment of the U.S. textile industry in the 1820s, were the staple textiles for domestic use for "sheeting" and "shirting" fabrics. Museum samples of these white goods

Figure 26 Mahatma Gandhi spinning. Photograph from the public domain, photographer unknown (https://commons.wikimedia.org/wiki/File:Gandhi_spinning.jpg).

resist identification because there is nothing obviously "Indian" about them. It is very likely, however, that a great many late eighteenth- and early nineteenth-century cotton textiles in U.S. museum collections are Indian (Bean 1990, 46). These imports created great wealth for textile merchants, who in turn invested profits in U.S. textile mills. Their ventures, along with their English production counterparts, eventually outcompeted the Indian market, putting Indian handweavers out of work, the very weavers whose plight eventually captured the eye of Gandhi (46). As Kenneth Ames (1985) aptly notes, linking weaving with a nostalgic ideal not only recalled a historical period but is a phenomenon that has continued with impressive vitality.

So, as the connotations of the spinning wheel and home spinning have varied over time (and space), so have the meanings of the term *homespun*. By 1765, the term—which then simply meant cloth made domestically—had already acquired national significance when the revolutionary activist group the Daughters of Liberty began holding spinning bees meant to serve as political gestures of self-reliance against English control of imported goods and industrial growth. This patriotic political-aesthetic was reinforced during the nineteenth century, particularly in southern states when yeoman farm wives, taking a cue from ideas advanced by both Washington and Jefferson, engaged in domestic cloth making, first as a gesture of nationalism in the wake of the War of 1812, and then in opposition to encroaching plantations, whose agricultural, political, and financial power was unassailable.

Although much of the fabric used in the early colonial period was either imported from Europe or produced by professional male weavers, spinning yarn and weaving cloth became an important visual element of America's origin myth, which is why homespun cloth as a material slogan of virtuous independence has taken on so many forms throughout our nation's history (Ulrich 2001). The widespread appearance of overshot coverlets in association with the yeomanry in piedmont Georgia today is testament to this association.

A Different Picture

Other documents in the Jackson archives paint a somewhat different portrait of the sisters' lives than that drawn by Myrick. Most of the letters were handwritten in cursive, and none was written by any of the sisters.[9] All letters were written to one or more of the Jacksons and were

Figure 27 "At Home" display of yeoman life, Madison Morgan Cultural Center, Washington, Georgia.

mostly from family members and friends about the weather, health, gossip about friends and relatives, and crops. Rare references to spinning or weaving gave little insight into when or to what extent, if any, the sisters were regularly involved in these activities. For example, in 1905 Cousin Lillie accuses the women of being too industrious and suspects that "after the crops are put up, [you] will not rest but start spinning and weaving."[10] It is hard to know whether these words were meant to be taken literally or were meant as poetic complements of the sisters' general industriousness.

Knitting, socks in particular, is mentioned in letters and receipts in the archive more often than spinning. It appears that some of the sisters occasionally knitted everyday goods like socks, either for sale or for trade. The cotton they used for this intermittent knitting work was purchased, rather than produced, much less spun, on their own property. Cotton yarn, for example, was purchased on October 24, 1916, from the Juliette Milling Company, as evidenced by a receipt in the collection.

On the other hand, the high value placed on the weaving arts by the Jackson sisters themselves is shown by materials in the collection. In fact, there were several weaving drafts for overshot coverlets signed by members of the Jackson family, such as Margery Jackson's "The Gentle Man Fancy" and "Soldier's Return" (fig. 28). Indeed, yeoman weavers often made modifications to patterns, and the individualized drafts were then kept as signed assets in family papers.

Because of the wide availability of factory-made goods like socks and bed coverings, weaving and spinning were not necessary to the procuring of household textiles for most U.S. families by the time the Jackson sisters caught the eye of journalists like Susan Myrick, who chose to portray them in the role of colonial homesteaders. But this angle was not unique to the *Macon Telegraph*. Some of the sisters' letters reveal that nonregional publications had even earlier promoted the sisters' lifestyle with all of its attendant accoutrements, including handspun cotton and woven bedcoverings. A letter from a Mrs. Walter Payne to Julia Jackson and her sisters suggests as much.

In her May 4, 1924, letter, Mrs. Payne explains that she has seen the story of the sisters and their "active lives" in a flyer left at her door.[11] Notably, this door was in Dallas, Texas, nearly nine hundred miles from the sisters' home. Channeling the emerging cultural practice of celebrating handmade artifacts of a bygone day, Payne writes to ask the sisters

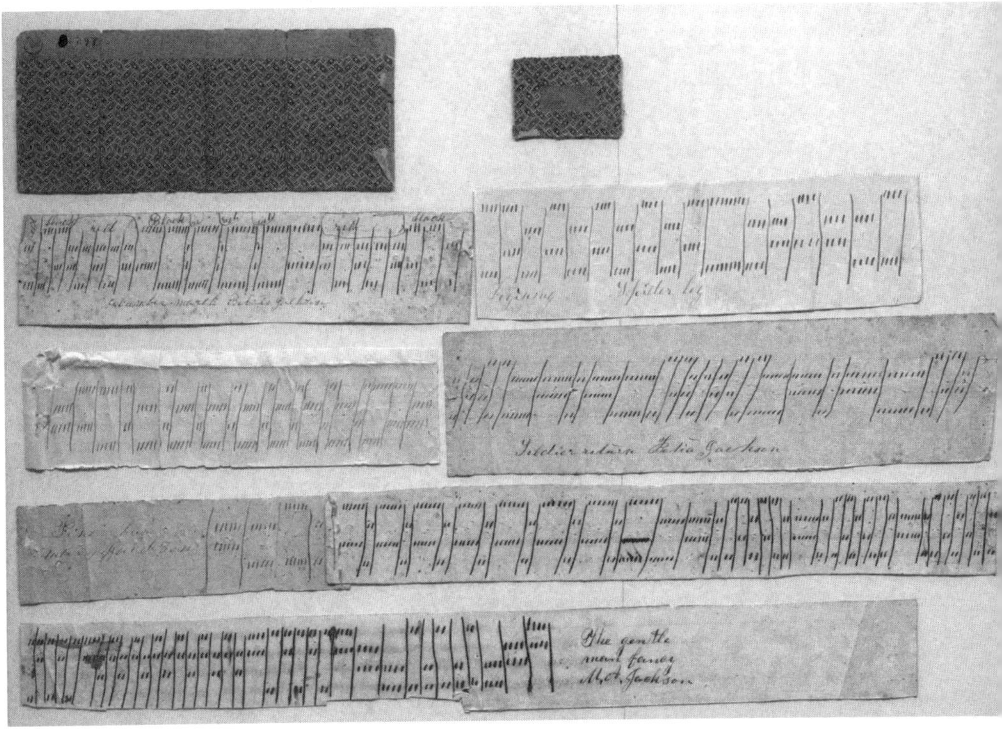

Figure 28 Signed weaving drafts. Courtesy Jackson Sisters Family Papers, acc. 1970-0297M, Georgia Archives.

if she can buy their coverlets and dishes so that she can stage her home so that it looks “old-fashioned.” Payne means to use objects to evoke the past as a matter of studied retro style rather than to stand as art or as fine material culture.

Another stranger from afar, a Mrs. H. B. Speed, also wrote to the sisters in response to an article circulated in her area. The article in question appeared in a newspaper circulated in Halsell, Alabama. In her November 8, 1927, letter, Speed tells about undergoing “the change” (menopause), then goes on to describe her interest in the sisters’ weaving and spinning. She admits to having never seen anyone weave, but mentions that her mother (b. 1846) had often spoken of weaving with her own sisters. Inspired by these accounts, Speed expresses a desire to acquire some “quilt patterns” and awaits correspondence from “each and every one of you.”

By saving these letters, the sisters clearly valued external interest in their lives. The letters support the sisters’ claim, as reported in Myrick’s article, that “folks had been coming there a wantin’ to buy things” (1929, 6). Perhaps it is not surprising that these sisters would have been “discovered” by people outside of their own community in the 1920s, since their skills and lifestyle choices were of especial interest to Myrick and to others in Myrick’s twentieth-century world.

Though the 1929 article suggests that it was her first visit to the sisters’ home, Myrick had already been seeking out rural folk of Middle Georgia for her articles. It is possible that Myrick had heard of the sisters as early as in 1912, when she was a schoolteacher in Round Oaks, Georgia (Krom 2003b). In her diary chronicling this time, Myrick deploys a backwoods tone that foreshadows the storytelling style of her 1929 article, describing, for example, “woodburning stoves to stoke and cracks in the walls of the room through which wind whistled mightily in the winter months” (quoted in Lindsley 2011, loc. 1606, Kindle). Her diary also depicts children sharing a single dipper to fill their buckets at the spring and quaint unpaved streets that she walked every day from her boarding room to the schoolhouse.

It is important to note that Round Oaks had become a stop on the Macon–Monticello railroad line in 1885, that the town was large enough to host an agricultural fair sponsored by the Grain Growers Club in 1900, and that the drafty schoolhouse was brand-new the year that Myrick began teaching there (Krom 2003a). Of course, the Jackson sisters would have been a well-known, long-standing family in this community when Myrick was there.

Even at an early age Myrick was an avid storyteller. Myrick's biographer, her niece Susan Lindsley, states that according to family legend, Myrick began both her storytelling and performing career at age five, when she was discovered reciting Uncle Remus's regional favorite, *Br'er Rabbit*, in the dialect of a "hired man" to a group of women and children in a clothing store while her mother shopped (Lindsley 2011). In a 1957 tribute to Myrick, *Atlanta Constitution* editor Reg Murphy described her passion for "the people"; in her own words, Myrick's love of Middle Georgia "just comes naturally. . . . I always say I was born and bred in a briar patch, and the first thing I can remember is riding two-on-a horse across the fields [at the Dovedale Plantation] with my father" (Murphy 1957). It would be some time before she had the chance to integrate these values into a professional career.

After graduating from Georgia Normal and Industrial College (now Georgia College and State University), Myrick taught school for ten years, taking time off for advanced studies in physical education at the American Medical Missionary College in Battle Creek, Michigan, and then at the Harvard University Summer School of Physical Education. She entered her journalism career in 1924 with her "Saner Eating" column in the *Macon Telegraph*. Her popular "Life in a Tangle" column later advised young women on matters of life and body under the pseudonym of Fannie Squeers (after the luckless-in-love Dickens character in *Nicholas Nickleby*). By 1928 she was a full-time reporter. Myrick eventually became the editor of the paper's Georgia Magazine section, in which the article about the Jackson sisters appeared (Grimes 1985, 198).

She stayed with the *Macon Telegraph* for fifty years, serving as war editor during World War II and farm editor in 1950. Myrick's support of rural farmers was recognized by the Woman of the Year in Agriculture Award from the *Progressive Farmer* journal and by a special citation from the National Association of Soil and Water Conservation Districts. After retiring in 1967, Myrick continued writing biweekly columns; even these were nostalgic pieces that revisited relevant articles on specific dates. In April 1969 she "looked back" to her article of May 1929, calling readers together with a remembrance: "people still talk of the Jackson Sisters."

Without a trace of irony, Myrick revisits the spinster story, a tale of women boldly fending for themselves, "eking out a living much like their pioneer ancestors had. They refused to have the aid from any man," took care of all aspects of the farm; they spun the cotton and wove cloth for their clothes, and spent spare time working on "bedspreads worthy of a museum" (Myrick 1969).

But this time Myrick had the advantage of looking through the artifacts that had ended up in Mrs. Wynnes's possession. Myrick describes a white work homespun spread, "embroidered with a replica of the American eagle; it looked as if the bird had alighted from a presidential seal" (Myrick 1929). With the inclusion of this detail, she firmly establishes the Jackson sisters as patriots in post–Civil War united America.

Woven with the Art of a Roy Crofter

Since Myrick was far more interested in and knowledgeable about agricultural practices than domestic crafts, it is curious that she focused her Jackson sisters articles around the vernacular handcrafts despite the sisters' statements that they had given up these practices because farming required all of their time and energy. Granted, as McCurry (1995) points out, the pre–Civil War trend of minimizing a woman's role in the field by highlighting her domestic virtues remained in place well into the twentieth century, but here was Susan Myrick, an independent modern woman—unmarried, highly educated, and professional—seemingly overintrigued by these handcrafts.

These points nagged at us until we revisited Myrick's 1929 article, and one line leaped out at us.

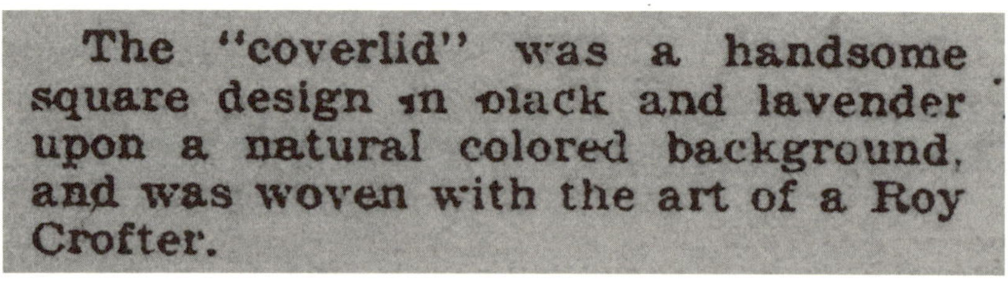
The "coverlid" was a handsome square design in black and lavender upon a natural colored background, and was woven with the art of a Roy Crofter.

Figure 29 Detail, "Five Sisters Lead Pioneer Lives" (1929), Susan Myrick. Image courtesy of the *Macon Telegraph*.

Although it needs to be unpacked, this single sentence points to the global context that connects Susan Myrick, the letters from Payne and Speed, the Jackson sisters, and coverlet weaving. The upshot is that depictions of the sisters as emblematic of an authentic life are happening in lockstep with a larger craft revival. And the popularization of the craft revival dovetailed with other aesthetic movements, some of which had an international scope with overtly political underpinnings. The Arts and Crafts movement, inspired in part by a critique of industrialized production, is a case in point.

William Morris's Arts and Crafts boutique-style printing press, critique of mass production, revaluation of women's labor, and romanticized love of folk craft influenced the American colonial revivalism we see glossed by Myrick as Roy Crofter. But why would Myrick use this term?

The figure most closely associated with Roycroft is Elbert Green Hubbard (1856–1915). Although today many people may not have heard of him, Hubbard was a "major superstar of his age" (Oberg 1994, 77). Hubbard and his suffragette wife, Alice Moore Hubbard, established the Roycroft community in East Aurora, New York, in 1895 following a trip to England, where he was inspired by William Morris's publishing practice and his Arts and Crafts philosophy. In fact, the U.S. press occasionally referred to Hubbard as "the William Morris of America" (Koch 1967, 73).

Morris had adapted ideas presented by Ruskin and Marx. Ruskin had castigated classical styles as mechanistic, criticized industrial capitalism, and venerated the decorative handiwork of medieval architecture (Weingarden 1985, 8). So, in conceptualizing a connection between artistic processes and the means of production within a particular socioeconomic base, Morris renovated techniques of medieval handicraft as a means of aesthetic and then political reform (8).

As a founding member of the Socialist League (1884), Morris was sympathetic to Marx's and Engels's critiques of the deleterious effects of alienated labor required by industrial production on both worker and product, and thus berated machine-made, mass-produced household artifacts associated with dehumanized, dehumanizing labor. Morris's solution was to identify a set of craft values that would undo the alienation of creative labor through making with pleasure and that was transparent in its production and use (Weingarden 1985, 9–10). The Roycroft creed follows this line of thinking (taken from Ruskin): "A belief in working with the head, hand and heart and mixing enough play with the work so that every task is pleasurable and makes for health and happiness" (Eisenstadt 2005, 1340). But influenced as he was by Morris, Hubbard was a fiercely independent-thinking autodidact and a thoroughly American entrepreneur. He was inspired by the methods and trappings of the Art and Crafts movement but was a champion of big business.

By 1900, Hubbard employed over two hundred Roycrofters who worked as metalsmiths, carpenters, graphic artists, writers, leathersmiths, weavers, artists, and bookbinders. His catalog for that year advertised not only books and furniture, but also rag carpets, "the old-fashioned kind—woven Roycroftie—stout, durable, beautiful—in East Aurora by Roycroft girls—seventy years young" (Koch 1967, 72). By 1914, he was also selling quantities of lamps, vases, desk sets, handbags, pillows, and table decorations in stylized art nouveau designs that were characterized as "choice, peculiar and unique things" (73).

Hubbard had survived the sinking of the *Titanic* only to perish in the sinking of the *Lusitania* in 1915.[12] His son, Elbert Jr., who turned out to be a substantially less nimble leader, took over Roycroft until it closed in 1938, by which time the books and objects that had been produced there had lost their appeal and were generally neglected and relegated to attics or secondhand stores. In the contemporary turn of the craft revival, Roycroft goods are again being collected as examples of American art characteristic of the late nineteenth and early twentieth centuries (Koch 1967, 82).

So by all accounts, Hubbard was a cultural figure of towering influence. The Roycroft Inn hosted thousands of visitors, some of them rather famous themselves (Oberg 1994, 79). Hubbard's books, community, and popular periodical, the *Philistine*—which advanced a somewhat kooky blend of critique, doctrine, and wit and affords a wide-ranging record of U.S. thought during the transition from the Victorian era to modernity—were familiar to Americans and taken up across sundry domains during the early twentieth century (White 1986, 83). For example, "Dog's Wool," an article appearing in the fanzine *Dogdom* in 1920, suggests forming a Roycroft-style industry to make dog hair yarn for an isolated mountain trail settlement of spinners who possess the rare qualities of those living so close to nature (Bechmann 1920).

So, though Hubbard died before Myrick began writing for the *Macon Telegraph*, by the 1920s, the Roy Crofter trope was emblematic of the kind of excellent, authentic artisanship that meshed with the American craft revival. By attaching an image of the Jackson sisters to "Roy Crofters," Myrick places the sisters and their work within this larger milieu.

Re-revivals

Like the eighteenth-century spinning activists before them, yeoman women continued to produce homespun objects for the same reason that supporters of the late century colonial revivalists staged spinning wheels in front of the hearth: spinning and spinning wheels were deployed to embody "the virtuous housewife who demonstrated both her love of home and her ability to conserve family resources through making various household items, both decorative and practical" (Casto 2006, 324). In the twentieth century, self-sufficiency was again signaled by displaying historic artifacts and their recreations. The photograph of the Jackson sisters with spinning wheel in front of coverlet is a case in point.

As we discuss in the next chapter, American colonialist revivalism emerged during the Depression and then again in the 1960s as exemplified by the publication of books like John Crosby's *The Forgotten Rebel: Gustav Stickley and his Craftsman Mission Furniture* and in exhibitions such as Princeton University's *American Arts and Crafts, 1876–1916*. After reviewing the archive in light of these recurring revivals, we concluded that the Jackson sisters were rather savvy, complicit purveyors of a retro image being advanced elsewhere as a larger U.S. craft revival that was a rerun of yeoman life between 1820 and 1860. And while antebellum coverlet production did have its own political aesthetic, yeoman weaving was an imagined, nostalgic reiteration of earlier times.

This revivalism reverberates today in yet another case of, as Yogi Berra put it, déjà vu all over again. Of course, the technical and labor landscape today is shot through with globalized production and consumption circuits, virtual imaging, and segmented labor processes that make the nascent industrial production of the nineteenth and early twentieth century look quite tame. But the promotion of handweaving as part of a larger critique of technology and alienated labor is alive and well. Examples of the coverlet as political aesthetic can be found in DIY crafting, top-selling books like *Handmade Nation* (Levine 2008), in Etsy-style making and selling, and even in the fine arts. Artists like Josh Faught, for example, use the techniques and surfaces of handcrafted textiles to investigate sublimated anxieties, the hidden politics of labor, and the visualization of subaltern identities. Though his weaving work is studied, Faught's work is associated with the Sloppy Craft movement that is a contemporary deployment of craft to highlight the human touch and an emotional connection to handwork and materials (see plate 10). This movement articulates with today's DIY movement and draws on themes from the school of Arts and Crafts.

As in the Jackson sisters' era, the current craze for handmade crafts succeeds in part through appealing to a sentimental desire for artisanal goods in the face of intensified globalized labor and technology, inexpensive machine-made imports, and a perceived loss of local attachments. Viewed in this light, the story of the post–Civil War Jackson family starts to look much less like traces from a "past agone" and much more like a quintessentially modernist episode in a long line of craft revivals and re-revivals.

Chapter 5 An Optical Art

> In visual art, there are two important elements: 1. boundary formations and the tease of the familiar, and 2. the poetics of color. I am juggling both of these visual quests for the past 60 years and I am finding echoes throughout history of these same concerns.—JULIAN STANCZAK (in Sherwin 2007)

How have coverlets been used to support, or even advance, contemporary cultural agendas or political ideas? How was a powerful symbol of "times agone" integrated into forward-looking frameworks of modernity? We have already seen how traditionalists like Susan Myrick and the Jackson sisters worked to advance a nostalgic interpretation of the woven coverlet form, at times positioning themselves against a self-consciously reflexive, modernist orientation that others would spearhead. And coverlets did, after all, always imply a utilitarian function. But that the artisanship of the patterning remains hidden until a coverlet is unfurled combined with the fact that coverlets were not all that warm suggests that their value for twentieth-century traditionalists was derived from properties beyond the functional. These semiotic features, the sign values, of the overshot woven coverlet—aesthetic, political, and cultural—were only selectively brought forward by revivalists as they sought to bring coverlets along from earlier eras.

In this chapter we examine how the visual patterns intrinsic to the overshot structure practiced by yeoman weavers eventually aligned, somewhat serendipitously, with the sensibilities of op art, a mid-twentieth-century movement recalling the future-looking constructivist period of the Bauhaus. The overshot aesthetic minus its yeomanesque political entailments was eventually reintroduced into contemporary art, particularly in the domains of painting, drawing, and of course, fiber art. Once again, as a boundary object that "is both plastic enough to adapt to local needs and the constraints of the several parties employing them, yet robust enough to maintain a common identity across sites" (Star and Griesemer 1989: 393), overshot inhabits competing, but companionable twentieth-century worldviews.

Oscillating Values

We observed that registrars, docents, curators, collectors, and others in charge of staging plantation houses and sites had a strong tendency to associate coverlets with children and enslaved Africans. Coverlets were thus implicitly framed as less interesting, less valuable, and the result of less skill than quilts or embroidered goods and other textiles routinely placed in masters' quarters. As coverlets connote a kind of old-fashioned and durable hominess (see chapter 2), this placement practice represents a rhetorical attempt to soften the realities of slave life. The rare coverlets placed in masters' rooms were folded into small volumes, minimized on the end of a bed as an accent, placed on the floor, or stuffed into armoires.[1]

In fact, the first colorfully patterned coverlet we saw displayed in affluent spaces as fine art—either unfolded on a master bed or hung vertically on a wall—was the Acacia Collection's red coverlet on loan to the Owens-Thomas House (see plate 11). At times docents allowed us to rearrange exhibits slightly to dramatic effect, such as a bold geometric pattern unfurled on a master bed.

We made these interventions not only as a design experiment but also as a way to visualize Sumpter Priddy's (2004) argument that mid-eighteenth-century fashion practiced by the middling classes prized color, pattern, ornament, and fanciful design that activated the senses and the imagination. Bold, overshot coverlets were part of this larger aesthetic trend. American Fancy with a capital F, as Priddy defines it, privileged novelty, optical qualities, and a spiritual dimension that Priddy writes reflected a shift toward an earthier Godhead.[2]

And while of course not every southern weaver in the time period he identifies was involved in Fancyness, we can assume that some were responding to, if not outright aspiring to this aesthetic preference. And like other trends that started in urban centers and then found purchase in rural areas, we would expect for American Fancy, really as a matter of taste, to have been extended for some time beyond Priddy's 1820 demarcation, especially in places where industrial production had not significantly challenged artisanal work and where the clean look of Gothic revivalism failed to take root.

None of the house museums or rooms in historical societies we saw were outfitted in this Fancy style—which by today's standards would look dazzlingly postmodern.[3] House re-creations for eighteenth- and nineteenth-century elite and yeoman families in Georgia typically reflect a staid, nostalgic version of the past that underplays racialized and political differences while using coverlets to connote hominess, resourcefulness, or self-sufficiency. Revivalists too have been selective in their readings of overshot weaving.

Traditional Chic

While some revivalists longed for an imagined past, others positioned overshot weaving within a quintessentially forward-looking worldview, a move that had to do with the formal qualities of overshot rather than its historical meanings. What is striking is how some proponents, like Frances Goodrich, were able to do both by simultaneously appealing to larger cultural currents, one retrogressive, the other resolutely modern.

During the mid-nineteenth century, self-sufficiency was represented in the both the act and artifact of home production, as reflected in products on display in house museums meant to picture this time period. Thus the Atlanta History Center's Smith Family Farm is staged to depict a mid-nineteenth-century aesthetic; spinning wheels, looms, and coverlets are prominently featured. Materials related to weaving dominate house museum rooms in ways that would have severely limited circulation and movement had they actually been in use there. This is the case in Callaway Plantation's piedmont plain-style house, which although it was the family home until after the Civil War, is staged to represent an earlier period.

The art of coverlet weaving had significantly waned by the late nineteenth century, but a range of publications helped promote a reconnection with an American colonial past, in a sentimentalized version of the preindustrial world. Proponents of the colonial revival movement recommended, for example, that homemakers place their spinning wheels before the hearth to symbolize a preindustrial past and concomitant "domestic adulation of the virtuous housewife who demonstrated both her love of home and her ability to conserve family resources through making various household items, both decorative and practical" (Casto 2006, 324).[4] These ideas made sense within ongoing critiques of capitalist industrialization penned by William Morris and John Ruskin that were gaining ground in Europe (and eventually mobilized by Theodor

Adorno, Max Horkheimer, and other scholars associated with the Frankfurt School).

Along these same colonial revivalist lines, the art critic and Ruskinite Clarence Cook encouraged aesthetically minded Americans to capture the spirit of the past in his series of home furnishing articles written for the well-known *Scribner's Monthly: An Illustrated Magazine for the People*. By 1878, Cook's entire series was collected for publication and became a popular guide to interior furnishings; *The House Beautiful* (Cook 1878) objectified things like spinning wheels.

The aesthetic preferences exerted by educated, worldly writers such as Susan Myrick were couched within the colonial revival. But while Myrick promoted the appreciation of coverlets as symbolic of a past long gone, other markedly southern revivalists, among them William G. Frost and Frances Goodrich, focused their energies on using coverlet weaving more pragmatically. Frost and Goodrich were salvagers who sought to revive traditional weaving, a practice they viewed as a folk victim of industrialization. But these two, influenced by the likes of Ruskin and Morris, also had an eye on the commercial. They saw the potential of overshot weaving to generate revenue that could be used to help to solve timely American problems such as poverty in Appalachian communities. And it is here that we can best appreciate how woven coverlets were depicted as remnants of an authentic preindustrial past, but also, and somewhat paradoxically, positioned within projects aimed at integrating rural folk into a modernizing national, and indeed, global, cultural economy.[5]

Frost, Berea College's third president, began marketing mountain-woven coverlets to college donors outside the region around 1893, which according to the Arts and Crafts writer Allen Eaton marked the beginning of the Appalachian crafts revival. At least one scholar calls this move to reintroduce coverlet weaving to Appalachian women as creating a livelihood to replace what had been a survival skill of the eighteenth century Broomfield 2006).[6] That coverlet weaving was described in this context as a "survival skill" is striking since coverlets took a lot of time to make; in times of emergency, a plain-weave wool blanket or batted quilt would be easier and faster to produce, and much warmer if you have to make something by hand.[7] These mountain textiles were definitely, on the other hand, optically stimulating, and attractive as collectables to northern donor families.

Part of Frost's challenge, one that Goodrich would also meet, was that skilled overshot weaving had all but disappeared from the region by the time he became interested in it. As a response, Frost eventually brought in Anna Ernberg, a Swede who had immigrated to New York, where she taught weaving at Teachers College (now Columbia University) and at the Pratt Institute. She had also been schooled in contemporary art and design trends. Ernberg was tasked with teaching weaving and running the weaving program at Berea and selling the products to northern consumers.

Goodrich's work operated in dialogue with Frost and Ernberg. Born into a family of intellectuals and Presbyterian ministers in New York in 1856, Frances Goodrich attended the Yale School of Fine Arts School (1879–82), where, as a woman, she was entitled only to a certificate of attendance. Influenced by the settlement movement in New York, Goodrich went to the mountains of North Carolina in 1890 to work for the Presbyterian Home Mission Board. Her mandate there was to elevate the standard of living for local women by "looking after" their educational and spiritual needs (J. Davidson 1989).

When a coverlet was given to her as a thank-you gift for her work in the community, Goodrich was not only touched by the gesture but inspired by the aesthetic of the weaving. On a trip north, she showed it to potential customers. Returning to North Carolina, she began to seek out coverlets and drafts across the region. She translated the draft notations that she found into a more modern-looking watercolor format. Goodrich marked her favorites, which were eventually included in what became known as her "Brown Book." In a reprinted version of Goodrich's book of drafts, the twenty-first-century editors romantically describe how "Miss Goodrich worked the beautiful patterns by the flickering light of her kerosene lamp on hand-made graph paper. First with pencil, then filling in with watercolor brush for the lovely drawdowns she created" (Miller and Schillo 2014, 14).

Selecting her favorite patterns, Goodrich designed overshot woven products (many of which were modified for the market) to be sold through the Presbyterian Church in a mail order system. In 1908, she opened her Allenstand Cottage Industries in Asheville, North Carolina, to sell locally crafted goods. Later in life she helped found the Southern Mountain Handicraft Guild, known today as the Southern Highland Craft Guild.

Goodrich also developed a process of "putting out," that is, segmenting the various steps in production. Jan Davidson (1989) points out that Goodrich replaced the traditional method of one-family production with a system involving multiple members of a community. From Goodrich's perspective, her method enabled more people to participate in the economic benefits of her enterprise, but from the point of view of a "revival," her methods were as much innovation as they were preservation (6–7). She made coverlet weaving into a commodity form created through a production regime that resembled an assembly line, which raised Appalachian peoples one step above the subsistence barter economy that had once characterized the region and one step closer to a cash economy and (the still insufficient) hourly wages to which many people there are now accustomed.

Meanwhile, in the world of images, Wallace Nutting, the Harvard-educated Congregational minister turned photographer, was capturing the imagination of the U.S. middle class with his carefully staged images of "Old America." An entrepreneurial synthesis of myth and materialism, Nutting's brand of imaginary colonialism appeared in hand-tinted photographs, on calendars, note cards, on the cover of magazines, and in his books. While his repertory was broad, the tableaus of costumed women advertised under the category of "colonials" proved to be his most lucrative subject. Nutting's iconic women took two forms: the productive (working women cooking, spinning, and sewing, often beside a cozy fire, to show that they are good mothers and wives); and the genteel (refined, elegant women of leisure, shown sitting and posed before their homes). The contradiction was solved in home decor; products offered by Berea College and Allenstand sold well to U.S. consumers, not unlike Mrs. Payne and Mrs. Speed, who were looking to add a colonial touch to their spaces of repose.

Until the end of World War II, writers and photographers continued to ponder the contradictions between the romantic past and the modernizing world; here, the acts and artifacts of spinning and overshot weaving could be used as powerful symbols of a bygone day. For example, the photographer Doris Ulmann, like Susan Myrick and Allen Eaton, was interested in documenting communities before their lifeways disappeared (though as a member of the pictorialist movement, her work was more aesthetic and artistic than journalistic or scholarly).

In a related academic vein, salvage ethnography was being developed by Franz Boas and his students during the early decades of the twentieth century at Columbia University, where Ulmann and her husband were then students. Most practitioners of salvage ethnography used the method of participant observation (in which researchers spend time with the communities they are studying) to record information about people whose ways of life were threatened either by colonization or modernization (or both). And while many early salvage studies were aimed at Native American populations, salvage ethnography was also deployed in other fields of study (ethnomusicology, folklore, photography, etc.).

During the 1920s, this paradigm was popularized outside of the academy by ethnographic filmmakers, among them Robert Flaherty. His 1922 groundbreaking *Nanook of the North,* a film version of pictorialism, what we might now call docudrama, depicted the disappearing Inuk tribe of Canada. *Nanook* was a major box office success and promoted the recording of rituals, customs, and faces of people vanishing from the world as a result of modernization. Many salvage ethnographies, such as those by Robert Flaherty or Edward Curtis, the famed photographer of Native Americans, were spiced with artistic license, based on secondhand accounts, and included staged scenes of inappropriately costumed subjects. They were also commercial, aimed at educated white American consumer audiences interested in themes of nostalgia, exoticism, and otherness. In the Southwest, a general interest in retaining a romantic notion of the disappearing native was expressed in the reinvention of Indian artisanry and linked to tourism and train lines. The commercial salience of these practices helps to explain the rise of artists like Doris Ulmann and her academic partners.

Along with Margaret Bourke-White, Ulmann was trained by Clarence White. Like Curtis and White, who carefully posed the subjects of photographs to evoke a specific idea, truth, or feeling, Ulmann was known to have captured the past by having people perform outdated tasks while dressed in antiquated costume. She photographed many Georgians, but in 1932, Ulmann began documenting Appalachian folk arts and crafts for Allen Eaton's masterful *Handicrafts of the Southern Highlands* (1937) (fig. 30). Eaton, like Elbert Hubbard, was a staunch proponent of the craft revival, salvage work, and commercial ventures. Again, we see especial value attributed to spinning and weaving as a primitive but authentic craft that is at once womanly, rural, premodern, and beautiful.

Eaton's book, subtitled "with an account of the rural handicraft movement in the United States and suggestions for the wider use of handicrafts in adult education and in recreation," features photographs and descriptions of Appalachian artists and their work. But Eaton's interest went beyond promoting a kind of democratization of art where fine and folk expressions were placed on a level playing field. His work was also fueled by an explicit political incentive: he believed that he could promote tolerance and pluralism in the United States through art, especially in the folk arts of denigrated and persecuted groups. In this, Eaton valued artistic expression for its ability to "communicate the plight of the poor and disaffected and to increase public awareness of a destructive political system that keeps power in the hands of a few" (Speer 1989, 226–27). Of course, as we have seen in the work on Frost and Goodrich, coverlets and overshot weavers fit easily within the paradigm of rural folk craft that was set against the fine (or aristocratic) arts and imbued with a kind of primordial U.S. nationalism.

During the interwar period, artists, collectors, and dealers surrendered to something like a "folk art fever" (Jentleson 2013). The search for a uniquely American artistic heritage eventually lead to the creation of the WPA–Federal Arts Project Index of American Design meant to create a visual narrative of U.S. material culture and the preservation of an American past to be used by future artists and designers. Between 1936 and 1942, trained artists traveled the countryside, rendering in watercolor eighteen thousand decorative art objects from the colonial period through nineteenth century. Echoing a rather bourgeois idea about the difference between folk art and the "aristocratic forms," Constance Rourke describes the value of this work: "An unmistakable richness becomes clear as the arts of design in this country are surveyed with anything more than a cursory glance. Their strong diversity is further indicated by two major classifications, the folk arts, and what, because of their origins, may be called the aristocratic forms . . . the folk arts run all the way from homespuns and simple furniture and ironwork to the distinctive creative forms of the Pennsylvania German and those of the old Spanish Southwest in painting or sculpture" (2003, 2).

Problematic in its underpinnings, folk art as defined by Holger Cahill, director of the WPA Federal Art Project, was made by common

Figure 30 *Aunt Lou Kitchen* (Shootin' Creek, North Carolina), Doris Ulmann (1933). Image courtesy of the Library of Congress.

people (like the plain folk of Georgia) with no formal arts training. Folk art like overshot weaving is then the "honest and straightforward expression of the spirit of the people" (2). This view of a simple art, wrought by joyful hands in an idealized past, disregards the cultural (or, in the case of coverlets, political and economic) context within which objects were made.

This ideal persists in the 2015 National Gallery of Art teacher's guide, where coverlet fragments are illustrated by artists like Ruth Barnes (see plate 12). A description of her illustration (watercolor and gouache on paper) of a woven fragment for the index is typical: "Woven coverlets, or bed coverings, were, perhaps, the most handsome products of both the housewives and the journeymen weavers. . . . The overshot weft threads . . . create variations in texture as well as pattern and produce the lively geometric surfaces that are characteristic of overshot coverlets. The patterns for these coverlets were largely traditional and were based on written drafts, or pattern guides, brought to America by European, English, and Scandinavian settlers. These drafts resemble musical notations, and, appropriately, the coverlets woven from them are, like this example, strikingly rhythmic in design."[8] During our research travels for this book we saw no examples of illustrations of fragments from coverlets said to have been made by slaves.

The degree to which revival textiles represent a straightforward expression of an authentic American people remains a question. In this case, the ends seemed to have shaped the means. The extent to which the woven goods—coverlets as well as other products that were made using overshot weaving—coming out of the Appalachian craft revival remained authentic in the way that promoters promised is questionable. For example, Ernberg imported looms from Sweden and then designed her own looms for Berea students.[9] She did this because her loom was smaller and easier to operate than those native to Appalachia, and it worked better with the special goods being designed and produced for sale. But the use of the Ernberg loom challenges the aura of authenticity surrounding these goods. David Whisnant labels this set of mountain goods driven by consumer taste as "traditional chic" (2009, 67) in his discussion of the impact of settlement school industries on Appalachian communities. And, it was middle- and upper-class consumers who were interested in using handmade goods and natural materials as a marker of style (and identity) in home decor but not in living an Appalachian lifestyle.

Of course, craft forms and methods are always subject to modification, and refusing to change them out of a stubborn attachment to an idealized past freezes practices into equally artificial museumifications. But given the massaging of image, of technique, and of design by pictorialist photography, the introduction of new looms and production methods, and the selection of products for sale by revivalists, one does wonder in just what way the revival coverlets represented an historical aesthetic.

Curator Lisa Dent at the Columbus Museum of Art commissioned a modern work to complement the museum's coverlet collection from the nineteenth century. In her craft installation there titled *Pattern Migration* (2011), the artist Stephanie Syjuco (n.d.) riffs off the coverlets in the museum's collection to generate hybrid forms "that address the friction between globalized production and artisanal craft" as well as frictions with immigration and consumption (fig. 31; see also plate 13). She describes her project: "Working with three contemporary weavers in the U.S. and Europe . . . , I had them each produce a new textile in the distinctive plaid pattern adorning cheap Chinese-made travel bags. Commonly used around the world, these bags are hallmarks of a globalized spread of objects, moving along with migrant communities. Working with a Chinese factory, I also produced five kilometers worth of plastic woven fabric, this time embedded with an American starburst pattern developed by a 19th Century weaver" (Syjuco n.d.). The new Chinese shopping bags act as hybrid objects linking nineteenth- to twenty-first-century contexts. Her work is a stunningly succinct example of the way that visual grammar can be mobilized within different political aesthetic regimes to highlight the paradoxical dynamics of continuity and disjuncture that mark globalization.

Scholars writing along these same lines of critique have shown how culture has been framed in terms of a sentimentalized past and then coopted for symbolic production, while commercialism destroys any genuine vestiges of remaining folkways (see Batteau 1979; Falls and Smith 2009, 2011). Whisnant and others who critique the commodification of Appalachian folk traditions charge that marketing to the tastes of middle-class America forever altered the traditional crafts. What emerged in this context was a hybrid, "a combination of some traditional colors,

Figure 31 Detail, *Pattern Migration*, Stephanie Syjuco (2011). The installation included 5 kilometers of plastic fabric printed in China with a nineteenth-century American coverlet pattern. Commissioned by the Columbus Museum of Art, Ohio (curator Lisa Dent).

processes and designs blended with alien (Swedish, for example) design features and materials, the whole applied to new products rarely if ever seen in mountain homes, such as cloth napkins, table runners, and place mats" (Whisnant 2009, 67).

The use of photography, the cataloging of folk art objects, and opening of settlement schools and stores in the early decades of the twentieth century by influential, well-connected people like Eaton, Goodrich, Ullman, Cahill, and Myrick put coverlets and overshot weaving before the public eye (although it is worth noting that while mountain weavers and their artifacts were made into objects of fascination, there was no sustained attempt to do the same with communities representing the former yeoman classes of Georgia). Whether the settlement school projects and the promotion of overshot constituted an exploitation of mountain communities, worked to blur class lines to allow for a cultural exchange, or raised consciousness about inequality (or some complicated mixture of all three) remains somewhat debatable (Stoddart 2002, 18; see also Tice 1998 and Batteau 1979). But mountain weavers and geometric overshot were undoubtedly framed as profoundly American.[10] The perception of overshot textiles as Americana along with the idea that Appalachian peoples embody the pioneer spirit of our nation's founding resonated with the public; as Woodrow Wilson put it, mountain residents represent "an unspoiled stock, stock of the original stuff of which America was made" (W. Wilson 1911).

This book examines the ways in which contemporary devaluations of overshot coverlets result in their placement in slave quarters in plantation settings. And yet, ironically, one of the reasons mountain folk were celebrated as resonating with revered seventeenth- and eighteenth-century American founders had to do with race. Though Berea College was initially an integrated institution, only a handful of nonwhite students were admitted in the pre–*Brown v. Board of Education* twentieth century. The supposed Anglo-Saxon heritage of Berea students and thus of their crafts even became a selling point with potential donors (see Whisnant 2009). In reality, romanticizing (and exceptionalizing) these mountain communities refracted a white nationalist mythos while masking the similar structural oppressions that existed between these whites with poor postwar whites and African Americans in Georgia and elsewhere (Batteau 1979).

Figure 32. The Wilson Bedroom at the White House (Washington, D.C.), circa 1915, with coverlet-inspired woven textiles. Image courtesy of the Library of Congress.

Images of primordial mountaineers stood side by side with stereotypes of Appalachians as backward feuders and moonshine makers, which champions like Frost, Goodman, Eaton, and even Woodrow Wilson worked to contradict, although some accounts suggest that Anna Ernberg exaggerated visions of Appalachian culture and squalor on her sales trips, perhaps as a way to conjure exoticism and raise donors' sympathies (Alvic 2015, 45). Revivalist coverlets were thus simultaneously framed as authentic relics and décor du jour. We cannot be surprised to learn that ordinary, seemingly middle-class women like Mrs. Payne and Mrs. Speed would be searching for samples of the overshot coverlet pattern featured not only in the constellation of rude trappings of the Jackson homestead but also in the Wilson Bedroom at the White House, where the carpet and upholstery clearly recall the woven coverlet (fig. 32).[11]

So as revivalists promoted social and political projects using weaving education and coverlet sales in poverty reduction schemes, it was the playful optical qualities of overshot that commanded the attention of the general consuming public and artists (particularly those moving toward an interest in illusion and abstraction). But why were worldly educators and artists so smitten with overshot coverlets? Could it be precisely because they presented as simultaneously primitive and modern? It is understandable, given her exposure to emerging global art trends, that promoters like Ernberg did not view coverlet weavers as cosmopolitan subjects but recognized that overshot coverlets might appeal to the contemporary eye.[12] Goodrich's training at Yale and her cosmopolitan northern and European contacts would also be brought to bear here in important ways. It was, after all, a time when line work, abstraction, the so-called primitivist movement, and interest in dissolving the art/craft distinction were being explored by well-known artists, whose work was snatched up by patrons.[13] The form of the overshot coverlet fit perfectly into this set of emerging political-aesthetic investigations.

Interpreting the Grid

The primitive-modern coverlet figured in yet another turn of the revivalist screw during the late 1930s and 1940s, when representatives from different schools of weaving debated the "correct" status of these objects. A well-known exchange between the Bauhaus trained weaver-artist Anni

Albers and the traditionalist Mary Atwater exemplifies the struggle between what Ed Rossbach identifies as "a desire to embrace the old ways and an eagerness to embrace the new" (quoted in Koplos and Metcalf 2010, 207). The issues playing out in the pages of the *Weaver* craft magazine were the value of overshot as a method of handweaving and as an aesthetic form.

Founded by Walter Gropius in 1919, the Bauhaus is probably best known in association with architecture, but its weaving and textile workshops were also significant (see Weltge 1993). In 1922 the Weimar government insisted, as a condition of the continuation of funding, that the Bauhaus stage a show of its work to demonstrate its accomplishments and suggest its sustainability. Pressures from the state led to the repudiation of some of the initial Marxist ideals advanced by Bauhaus leaders like Walter Gropius and a turn toward industrial design, mass production, and sales.

As Ben Davis (2010) puts it, the Bauhaus "was not just a school dedicated to creating attractive objects; its production is shot through with the luminosity of political passion. But . . . it is also important to see that this was *displaced* energy, responding to the right questions but unable to provide the answers to them on its own" because they were forced to respond to political pressures brought to bear by the rise of the Nazi party (original emphasis). The Bauhaus weaving workshop, turning out such famed makers as Gunta Stolzl, Anni Albers, Benita Otte, Otti Berger, and Marli Ehrman, became very successful under these new commercial terms.

As with the British Arts and Crafts movement from which the Bauhaus took inspiration, the weaving program privileged artisanal craftmanship. Weavers operated on the belief that excellent making resulted from a solid foundational practice, but their valorization of the handmade was combined with an ideology of high craft to create what they hoped would be an aesthetically rich textile, even when mass-produced and industrialized.

The Bauhaus curriculum assumed training in textile, weaving, and fashion to be on par with other artistic practices (painting, for example) to be approached after foundational work was mastered. Interestingly, even as the Bauhaus proclaimed gender equality, the educational policy at the Bauhaus itself enacted sexism, largely shunting women students into weaving and textile training.[14]

Figure 33 Collaborative coverlet woven by SCAD fiber students for *Fold Unfold*. SCAD Professor Jennifer Moss and students from "Introduction to Weaving," 2017.

So even as the Bauhaus was rooted in a critique of capitalism, casting the great crime of industry as the removal of the soul of goods, Bauhaus denizens recognized that the survival of the school depended on integrating an industrial approach to making and insisted that good designers could impart the hand through industrial means.[15] A modernist aesthetic combined with an investigation of form can be seen throughout Bauhaus work by painters Paul Klee, Wassily Kandinsky, Josef Albers, and others, and the same spirit would be taken up in the study of weaving.

Although the Bauhaus postdated the tradition of the Jeffersonian-era woven coverlets examined in chapter 2, that both embody a minimalist aesthetic, reject traditional, authoritative forms, and promote foundational self sufficiency and self-reliance is anachronistic but not coincidental. They each in their own way valued the competence and good virtue of everyday people, criticized rising industrial capitalism, and generated a pragmatic orientation to design. The commonalities in these political aesthetic philosophies—developed in their respective, separate contexts by European scholars and yeomen—came together in the hills of Appalachia to create the perfect home for the weaver-artist Anni Albers. Albers began teaching with her husband Josef Albers at the now-famed Black Mountain College in the 1930s after the Nazis shuttered the Bauhaus.[16]

There Albers rejected the idea of traditional formulas as things of the past while she celebrated the ancient progenitors of weaving itself. In investigating surface optics using a vocabulary of line and grid, Albers looked to the structure of weaving as a key to the medium's aesthetic possibilities, creating architectural rectangles out of bands and stripes. Later, Albers would apply these same principles to a paper practice. It is instructive to recall her observation that "if anything is on paper, it is seen as art, while there is great hesitation by galleries and museums to show anything made of thread" (quoted in Malarcher 1985). Her work, encapsulated in "Handweaving Today: Textile Work at Black Mountain College" (1941) was resolutely modernist and futurist: in that essay, Albers called for experimentation based on a study of structural foundations to move weaving further into the realm of the arts.

Mary Atwater's position stood in contrast to the philosophy of making espoused by Albers and other Bauhaus members. Associated in the public eye with overshot coverlets in the folk tradition, Atwater argued in her many workshops and publications for the pleasure of making and for the role of handmade textiles in adding comfort to everyday life. As a teacher, she also prized fidelity to historic patterns and promoted teaching through copying. This insistence on faithfulness to pattern countered the overshot weaving practice of women in the nineteenth century modifying patterns to make them their own. Woven objects from that era had a degree of uniqueness, at times resulting from error, but also clearly from intentional amendment to existing patterns or as sheer invention.

In "It's Pretty—But Is It Art?"(1941), penned in response to Albers's "Handweaving Today" and published in the same journal, Atwater disparaged experimental weaving as "free form," argued that machine weave lacked the qualities that made hand weaving attractive and endearing, and she vehemently rejected the idea that weaving could rise to the level of art. In Atwater's quintessentially preservationist approach, weaving should remain practical, hobbyist, and historical.

These seemingly irreconcilable positions were advanced in both print and practice, but in the following decades artists like California weaver Polly Yori found a third way. She taught traditional practices in nontraditional ways. Yori used what we might identify as a Bauhaus-like strategy of using paper and collage to create op art designs that were then reproduced using overshot technique. Work emerging from this third-way pedagogy, such as that by weaver Laurie Herrick, was intended for the wall and self-consciously artistic. Herrick's tricolored weaving *Three Giraffes* (ca. 1970), for example, brings to bear an interest in overshot and op art, and in Bridget Riley's work (e.g., *Movement in Squares*, 1961) we can see the affinity to an investigation of patterning and optical wonders.[17]

Contemporary responses to work by Herrick and Riley have included an overshot aesthetic but have often been rendered using digital imaging or loom technologies. These decisively contemporary wall works—for example Rosalie Neilson's *Op to Be Square* (a warp rep rug designed and woven to honor Laurie Herrick) or Christie Matson's sound and weaving work (fig. 34)—echo nineteenth- and even eighteenth-century overshot coverlets sourced from the Georgia piedmont.[18]

Possibly the most salient theme to emerge in woven textiles is the dynamic of concealing and revealing, especially as expressed in the over-under architecture of warp and weft exploited with such artistry in overshot work. Richard Tuttle compared this theme in weaving with

Figure 34 *Composition in Circle*, Christy Matson (2011). Photo by Matthew Miller, courtesy of Pacific Northwest College of Art.

the grid motif central to minimalist art and beyond (Petersens 2014, 78). Indeed, the coverlet shown in figure 35 was discovered by De Young textile curator Jill D'Alessandro and included in the aptly titled *On the Grid: Textiles and Minimalism* exhibit (2016), which examined the minimalist art aesthetic with regard to abstraction, precision, geometry, materiality, and process.[19] The circa-1960 coverlet at the De Young museum is reminiscent of the 1850 Georgian Lovelace fragment (see plate 14).

The overshot form relies on a relatively constant optic generated by the structure of loom, but it has also been embedded in at times competing responses to aesthetic, political, economic, and social conditions. So, while we challenge the relegation of coverlets in house museums to children's rooms, slave quarters, and the bottom of closets, we must also revise the easy conflation of "primitive" craft with hardscrabble rurality or hominess. By examining how both traditional and contemporary overshot exposes an underlying algebra of production, that is to say the grid and everything it implies, both literally and figuratively, overshot is shown as a nimble time traveler, an incredibly rich form that has always been evolving and modernist.

Figure 35 Op art *Coverlet*, ca. 1960, United States, cotton; double-weave, 233.7 × 166.4 centimeters (92 × 65½ in.), museum purchase, David and Susan Hodges Fund. Courtesy of Fine Arts Museums of San Francisco.

Chapter 6 Unfolded

A set of oppositional terms—slave versus master, primitive versus sophisticated, white versus black, rural versus urban, nature versus culture, and craft versus art—is advanced again and again in Georgian exhibits containing overshot coverlets. The surfacing of a story about a white rural woman handmaking fine, sophisticated textiles confounds these received categories, but it also provides clues to understanding how these objects have been mobilized in the service of other projects, giving contemporary overshot weaving (and the art that is derived from it) a rich salience.

Artpolitical formations are simultaneously abstract (as in values, ideologies, and preferences) and concrete (as in crafted objects, museum exhibitions, and language). The artpolitical, broadly conceived as a multimedia surround of both practices and material culture, is the environment in which agency is exerted, or constrained (see Sartwell 2010).[1] As a boundary object, the formal qualities of the overshot coverlet have remained somewhat constant, while its meaning changes, at times quite dramatically.

This book explores how coverlets have operated as props that soften the appearance of slavery by creating an impression of decorative coziness. This happens alongside the ongoing promotion of a Lost Cause narrative that underplays race, labor, and slavery. It is no coincidence that we often hear tour guides in these settings claiming that "the planter family treated their slaves extremely well" or that a family treated their slaves "just like family." Relatedly, we showed how yeomen women performed an imagined Jeffersonian political identity through the act of weaving within a rapidly industrializing and globalizing cotton economy. Some aspects of their practice were taken up in a craft revival linked to a burgeoning nationalist white Americana movement. Here, the nostalgic celebration of "times agone" were wedded to an attempt to identify a primordial character in the face of anxieties produced by economic woes and the loss of a connection to the local generated by global commodity circuits.

Interestingly, as the formal features of the coverlet—with its spectacular geometric variety—begin to align with explorations in vision, cognition, and digital machine science, the coverlet was ushered into a postmodern incarnation, a political episteme based on surface, reruns, intertextuality, performance, commodification, and late neoliberal capitalism (and all of its entailments) that we see addressed by contemporary makers. Some of this work, such as that by Rowland Ricketts, deals with matters of race and class, power, nationalism, and the production of southern history as narrative (fig. 36; see also plate 15).

It remains to be seen how dissent using the vocabulary of overshot and advanced within the white-box gallery system will be taken up by viewers, consumers, and critics of art and craft. What is certain is that analysis of the production and interpretation of overshot in contemporary art can reveal the critical seams and pressure points within capitalism

Figure 36 Detail, *Unbound* series 3, no. 1, Rowland Ricketts (2018). Indigo and madder-dyed wool, undyed wool (2017–18), 61 × 68 inches.

and class, labor and technology, and the grid as guiding metaphor and marker of modernity.

Yeomanwerk

In its current incarnation, the overshot textile form has been transferred from loom to machine or paper, where the translation from ideal pattern to material culture is more guaranteed. Viewed in this light, the coverlet is an aesthetic form based *in* the fiber arts, but it is also *about* fiber practices and their makers and, thus, is both a practice in and an index of globalization within a race and class-stratified, technology-rich United States.[2]

Scholars have long written about the ways in which the state typically serves the needs and interests of the ruling class, at times though interacting with public activities in churches, schools, sporting events, museums, art exhibits, and so forth. At times, less powerful groups work to advance the hegemony of the state (and the ruling class that the state serves), but they can also contest the status quo. The spaces where these values, attitudes, practices, and projects are negotiated are the institutions that Antonio Gramsci collectively referred to as civil society. And since the realm of civil society is where power is expressed, exerted, and contested, and since art and craft are the products of activities within it, we should be paying attention to art and craft as important facets of hegemonic and counter-hegemonic artpolitical systems.[3]

Overshot considers how material culture has been included in, or excluded from, antebellum history, exhibitions, and collecting institutions. The book grapples with the question of how and why exhibiting coverlets as slave goods came about in the first place, as well as why yeomen were edged from historical narratives. White yeoman culture is entirely absent in the interpretive staging of the antebellum South in coastal museums. Taken together, these practices inadvertently reproduce an exclusion having to do with class and "not-quite-whiteness," a term that reflects the inflections of class that mark the construction of whiteness as a racial category (see Wray 2006).

The antebellum yeomanry were unlike the contemporary middle class mainly because of their associations with industrialized labor. But like the middle class today, they were elided from popular and even scholarly accounts—perhaps for their very ubiquitousness. In Hollywood films, the projected world of the middle class is one that only about 15 percent of Americans could actually live in (K. Clark 2013). A tremendous amount of work in the social sciences concerns impoverished and marginalized populations, with some work focused on the elite (known as studying up), but far less research concerns the middle classes so crucial to the operations of U.S. society. Opening new questions on the material culture of the low-country yeomanry among women is part of a broader effort across the humanities to recapture this segment of the population, crucial for understanding an increasingly neoliberalized U.S. society.

Consider, for example, that between 1947 and 1973, real wages rose by 60 percent, but between 1973 and 1986 real wages fell by 14 percent. This trend was accompanied by a massive accumulation of wealth by the richest 5 to 10 percent of the population. Between 1995 and 2000, income for the top 0.01 percent increased 156 percent (Bluestone 2014). That there are powerful racial and gendered components to this increasing inequality goes without saying. The upward movement of wealth and consolidation of power has continued unabated through to the present, enabled by the restructuring of capitalism by Ronald Reagan and Margaret Thatcher and pursued with eagerness by subsequent U.S. presidential administrations (see Harvey 2005).[4]

That class inequality is increasing is just one of the deleterious consequences of this restructuring. A 1987 *Washington Post* article by labor lawyer Lance Compa still sounds mighty relevant three decades later: "Instead of a secure middle class we have an American working class whose wages are dropping, whose good jobs are disappearing and whose whole families have to work to make ends meet. Much of the vaunted middle class is looking at a future closer to the underclass nightmare than the American dream, but the unemployment figure on the nightly news remains the mark by which we measure the well-being of the people who actually do the work in this country, rather than those who simply devise new ways to profit from their investments" (Compa 1987).

As illustrated by the rise of the Tea Party and a subsequent victory by Donald Trump in the 2016 presidential contest, we see the reemergence of a selectively idealized Jeffersonian yeoman balking at the consolidation of power and wealth of the upper "one percent." Americans losing financial ground to the digital service economy seem to be longing for a self-sufficient racialized yeoman of the past, imagining themselves in opposition to the "planter" class (striking given Trump's own personal wealth, the irony of which has not been overlooked). Today's version of this shows white privilege being made explicit through claims to economic, political, and cultural opportunities and rights.

This new social imaginary—which is explicitly racist and nationalist—turns on a political aesthetic to which Trump appealed with his promise to "Make America Great Again" by bringing back working-class jobs, putting America first before other nations, deporting job-stealing not-quite-white immigrants, and undermining "liberal elites" who are blamed for corrupting politics.

So while yeoman weaving may have been motivated within a safety-first subsistence strategy and a critique of elite consumption practices, overshot coverlets also call attention to realms of agriculture, labor, consumption, distribution infrastructures, and everything in between, mirroring the mechanization of the cotton industry. Nothing is more central to this configuration than shifts in technology.[5]

Beyond the Grid

As we have shown, as production regimes changed, so did the meanings of the coverlet. Drawing on "The Fragment on Machines" (1857), an essay in which Marx describes technology as the capture of labor and skill that are then turned against the worker, we see coverlet weaving as an erstwhile critique of alienated labor during the industrial boom.

Today's cotton looms—and indeed the entire process of cultivating, harvesting, and processing cotton—are not just mechanical, they are digital. The person-to-product ratio has been sharply reduced to maintain only enough workers to keep the machines going. The radical potential, weak though it may have been, of overshot coverlets to cut against planter-class consumption habits and a rising industrialized textile industry with its machined, wage-labored goods was eviscerated when revivalists accentuated its formal and utilitarian qualities and the coverlet was commodified and then digitized. But to what end? Ironically, the yielding of the handweave to binary digitalism is precisely what makes overshot an excellent medium for artists like Allison Smith, Josh Faught, Christy Matson, and Stephanie Syjuco to successfully register a politics of dissent.

Severe constraints created by material availability and loom construction fueled an exploration expressed by the almost limitless permutations of tiny squares—pixels in today's vernacular. The binary 0-1 is the foundation of digital software; it is also staggeringly simple and constitutes the foundation for the grid. The most precise and revealing metaphor of contemporary U.S. society, the grid can also refer to both hard and soft infrastructures, from water and electrical pipes to ports and highways and franchised shopping, to more abstract phenomena like educational curricula, economic development paradigms, consumption norms, and ideologies about race, class, and gender. In all these contexts, "snapping to the grid" means avoiding ambiguity and erasing idiosyncrasy in order to align with hegemonic values.

The formal essence of the coverlet is also a (quintessentially modernist) grid.[6] However, museum settings powerfully deploy the coverlet to suggest—even if at times unwittingly—a primitive, premodern, even "off-the-grid" sensibility. And while what is viewed as on or off the grid shifts over time, being on the grid and being off the grid are not mutually exclusive. In fact, rhizomatic locations—being off the grid while on the grid, or, being on the grid while off the grid—are sacred, charged spaces where new landscapes can be forged.

Weaving is constrained, overdetermined even, by the strict loom structure, where opportunities for the appearance of the hand, an artist's individual presence, is reduced, especially when compared with the expressive arts such as painting, drawing, poetry, or sculpture. One might even say that the intense constraints of loomwork foster creativity in a way that free-form work does not. Members of artistic groups like Oulipo (Ouvroir de littérature potentielle) and Outrapo (Ouvroir de tragicomédie potentielle) have explored how constraints in literature and in the dramatic arts generate inventiveness.

But if we compare the work of a contemporary fibers artist like Liz Sargent to more regimented, neatnik coverlets, an initial dismissal of the coverlet as mechanical is understandable. Sargent's work is entropic and aleatory rather than tightly constrained by a technological principle. The structures of her work are decidedly conceptual (see fig. 38 and plate 16).

Unlike handweaving, mechanized looms and digital image programs are designed to pull everything into precise horizontal and vertical alignment, thereby eradicating, or at least minimizing, idiosyncrasy.[7] The contemporary eye, accustomed to smooth, computerized alignments, may even squint when things are misaligned.

Some artists have embraced "the glitch," a digital mistake that reveals an underlying binary framework. In their ethnography *Off the Grid*, Phillip Vannini and Jonathan Taggart argue that off-gridders—people living away from electrical or gas infrastructure—radically reinvent domestic life in houses that are experimental labs for a collective future (Vannini and Taggart 2015). Like artworks based on the glitch, such social experiments are epiphenomenal, opposed to but ultimately enabled by, and casting into relief, existing technological and cultural trappings.

So, to look forward by looking back, if we place yeoman women whose lives were marked by kind of off-the-gridness *avant la lettre* into a historical trajectory with Liz Sargent's work, we can suggest a different way of thinking about grid work as a site for critique. How do ideas about the grid mimic the ethos of a time period? Could it be that meaningful critique comes from embrace of rather than escape from the grid?

The grid, a visualization of the march toward the hegemony of mathematical calculation, is the central trope of western modernity and, as such, has both material and semiotic effects. In response to the 1811 imposition of the grid on New York City, Rem Koolhaas wrote: "The grid is above all, a conceptual speculation . . . in its indifference to topography, to what exists, it claims the superiority of mental construction over reality" (1978, 20). In recognizing the paradox of the grid, he described it as a "negative symbol of the shortsightedness of commercial interests" that traded the element of design and creativity for convenience. But subjugation to the grid can instigate and fuel a vertical ego of each block and generate, finally, a three-dimensional anarchy (Minca 2012).

Adolfo Natalini and Cristiano Toraldo di Francia's architecture collective Superstudio, founded in 1966, worked the grid as both democratic-homogenous and dystopic-terrifying, arguing that to speak of being "off the grid" necessarily speaks to the future as both critique and escape. In Superstudio's *Continuous Monument*, the grid extends infinitely everywhere.[8] Here, being on the grid and off the grid are not mutually exclusive (or even possible).

These both/and locations—*both* off the grid *and* on the grid, or *both* on the grid *and* off the grid—represent potential spaces of liberation. Vannini and Taggart ultimately show how people live on the grid while presenting themselves to the world as living off the grid. After all, aren't off-gridders who live in a trailer but occasionally shop at Walmart really just car camping on a really big scale? But what about living off the grid while presenting as on the grid? That position not only reflects the inevitable incompleteness of capture by the grid (demonstrated aesthetically by yeoman coverlets) but also shows how grids, as social structures and practices, fold and reticulate in unexpected ways. So, under what circumstances does off the grid / on the grid–ness mark progressive or escapist politics?

The stridently modern grid is the means of crowding out the dimensions of the real world and replacing them with the lateral spread of a single surface (Krauss 1965). In its formal essence, the coverlet is also a borderless grid, which is itself a symbol of fabrication denoting both convention and conservatism, a metaphor for social structures that expand into material ones such as power lines or trade routes.

But mechanized as they are, coverlets always show the hand of the maker, and so they also must operate as a powerful metonym for the ways in which the ideal of the grid is always troubled in the real world. The grid as a modernist imaginary is always disturbed, either on purpose or by accident. In many ways, the idea of a borderless grid has emerged to assuage the failure of modernity.

By simultaneously rationalizing the urban experience and allowing an irrational topography to reign, Superstudio's *Continuous Monument* is a mythological response to a nineteenth-century notion of grid that celebrates the logic of hierarchy and the law of excluded middles that was so eloquently expressed in yeoman textiles a century before.

Sargent's work, using deconstructed machined fabric represents a fiber form profoundly transfigured through the artist's hand. In *Into the Web* (fig. 38), the grid exceeds the worlds it defines, while submitting to topography and doubling on itself. Reading the grid through Sargent's work shows it now as heterarchical: think rhizome, hyperlink, virtual reality, and time-space compression (see plate 16).[9] These seem to be the principles on which contemporary societies are constructed or at least how they are theorized. Should not dismantling, or at least eroding, hegemonic power take the same form?

In fifteenth- and sixteenth-century treatises on perspective, then in studies by Paolo Uccello or Albrecht Dürer (see Krauss 1965), and now in work by Sargent, scholars and artists have considered how one reality might be mapped onto another by bending grids to will, exploiting the points of flexion. A pointedly heterarchical sociology suggests how to map one experience in terms of another: as Dougald O'Reilly wrote,

Figure 37 The ideal of the grid is always troubled in the real world: the presence of the artist is announced by off-grid grammar in hand-painted signage rendered by Leonard Miller (2008), Savannah, Georgia.

> Hierarchy is often perceived as the only alternative to egalitarian social relationships and the belief that if equal access to resources is not open to every individual then a hierarchy must exist. Heterarchy instead stresses the examining of relationships between institutions or individuals from a number of perspectives. . . . As conditions change so might the prevailing social order. Relationships must be conceived of as multidimensional rather than a unilateral, unidirectional flow of interaction. . . . The true value of heterarchy lies in its ability to embrace these truths and recognize the flexible and transient nature of human interaction. (O'Reilly 2003, 176; see also Falls 2017)

Here, the extent to which one operates "off the grid" while presenting as "on the grid" is largely a matter of perspective.

Like hashtag activists, students and faculty of the Free University of New York City, and the hacker group Anonymous, yeoman weavers were

Figure 38 *Into the Web*, Liz Sargent (2002). Original upholstery on furniture deconstructed; installation at Cranbrook Art Museum.

operating on a robust infrastructure promoted by the class in power and the authoritative state institutions that served them; but what they were doing was counter-hegemonic. These off the grid / on the grid critics inhabited interstices, highjacked infrastructures, and followed aesthetics that suited their own purposes, performing critique to local audiences. In opposition to living on the grid / off the grid, operating off the grid / on the grid is a nod to the future and to an optimistic belief in the ability of people to construct a world in their own image—to design, as it were, a different social, political, and economic landscape.

During our visit to museums and house museums, we often heard nineteenth-century woven coverlets described as mechanical cloth that fails to rise to the level of art. Collectors and auction houses often will not accept coverlets, the general consensus being that they have little or no value apart from sentiment. We beg to differ, mainly because overshot woven coverlets are not, and have never been, either-or objects. They are both/and objects. Coverlets are not either art or craft, either high or folk work, either primitive or modern, either aesthetic or functional, or either rural or urban-cosmopolitan—but rather *both* art *and* craft, primitive *and* modern, aesthetic *and* functional, rural *and* cosmopolitan. And herein lies the power of overshot.

Notes

Chapter 1 Setting the Loom

1 The one Smithsonian coverlet with a solidly southern provenance, "Braddocks Defeat Coverlet," is said to have been woven in 1833 by Lavina Rogers of Horse Creek, Tennessee. The description notes that "there were very few female hand-weavers in 1833. In most cases women spun the yarn used in their coverlets, and commissioned a professional weaver to actually weave the coverlet." See https://www.si.edu/sisearch/collection-images?edan_q=Lavina%2BRogers.

2 For more details about the Georgian landscape, see Mark V. Wetherington (2018), "Wiregrass Georgia," *The New Georgia Encyclopedia*, October 1, https://www.georgiaencyclopedia.org/articles/geography-environment/wiregrass-georgia.

3 Soffer, Adovasio, and Hyland (2000) show that these figures are not naked, but wearing finely constructed headwear, body bandeaux, and aprons or skirts. Carefully (and exquisitely) rendered in stone, these figures are striking in their premonition of ritual garments used throughout the world, and index sophisticated technological skills of Upper Paleolithic artisans as well as women's power, prestige, and value.

4 The AIDS Memorial Quilt project founder, Cleve Jones, cofounded the San Francisco AIDS Foundation in 1983 and the NAMES Project AIDS Memorial Quilt in 1987. See the AIDS Memorial Quilt website (http://www.aidsquilt.org/) for further information.

5 Twentieth-century revivalists often expected handweavers to match seams and follow production standards defined by a philosophy of industrial output, as opposed to the unique objects made by coverlet weavers of the nineteenth century.

6 See Falls 2017 for an extensive ethnographic exploration of breast milk as a boundary object.

7 Research for *Fold Unfold* was funded by a Craft Research Fund Grant from the Center for Craft, Creativity and Design (CCCD) and by the Savannah College of Art and Design. See details about the CCCD at http://www.craftcreativitydesign.org/2016-craft-research-fund-grants/.

8 In her study of pre-Columbian Andean textiles, French anthropologist Sophie Desrosiers (2012, 674) warns about the use of an ethnocentric lens, which impedes our understanding of how makers might have considered their work.

9 See the artists' websites for more detailed information: Allison Smith, https://www.allisonsmithstudio.com/a-b-o-u-t; Christy Matson, https://www.cmatson.com/; Stephanie Sujuco, https://www.stephaniesyjuco.com/projects/pattern-migration. On Josh Faught, see Elissa Auther (2016), "'He Is Survived by His Longtime Companion': Feeling in the Work of Josh Faught," *Art Practical*, February 26, https://www.artpractical.com/feature/he-is-survived-by-his-longtime-companion-feeling-in-the-work-of-josh-faught/.

Chapter 2 Said to Have Been Made by Slaves

1 See the "Owens-Thomas House and Slave Quarters" page at the Telfair Museums' website, http://www.telfair.org/visit/owens-thomas/, accessed February 1, 2017.

2 Acacia Collection website, www.acaciacollection.com (dead), viewed January 2015. The entire Acacia Collection was auctioned off in 2017. The auction catalog—*Slotkin Folk Art Auction Nov. 11–12, 2017: Slavery Freedom & Beyond*, October 3, 2017—appears at https://issuu.com/slotinfolkart/docs/slotinfolkartauctionnov2017catalog.

3 Projects such as Derek Alderman's Tourism RESET and the Slave Dwelling Project (http://slavedwellingproject.org/, founded by tour guide Joseph McGill) as well as recent books—see Kytle and Roberts (2018) and Levin (2018)—explore how confederate monuments, plantation tours, Hollywood movies, and historic preservation strategies have been used to whitewash histories of the antebellum South. Jason Silverstein (2018) aptly reads current events through these texts: "The plantation is the Rorschach test for America's soul: you either see moonlight and magnolias or a crime scene."

4 Mitchell's *Gone with the Wind* (1936) was chosen as one of eighty-eight books for the Library of Congress "Books That Shaped America" exhibit. The book received a Pulitzer Prize for Fiction in 1947 and the National Book Award in 1937. To date, more than thirty million copies of *Gone with the Wind* have been printed.

5 Susan Ogden, "Slave Quarters . . . Owens-Thomas House, Savannah, Ga.," *Flikr*, 2010, http://www.flickr.com/photos/captured_echoes/4495111625.

6 Stephanie Shaw's (2003) discussion of the debates surrounding the use of WPA narratives for historians and others is both fascinating and helpful.

7 States represented in the WPA *Slave Narratives* are Alabama, Arkansas, Florida, Georgia, Indiana, Kansas, Kentucky, Maryland, Mississippi, Missouri, North Carolina, Ohio, Oklahoma, South Carolina, Tennessee, Texas, and Virginia.

8 Labor performed by white plantation women in the field during this period tends to be underrepresented in written accounts; most yeoman farm wives actively participated in the preparation, maintenance, and harvesting of crops (S. Shaw 2003).

9 Arrington family archive (donated by Mrs. Alton Hill), Roswell Historical Society; viewed March 2015.

10 Historian Paul Pressley emphasizes that, until the Revolution, the vast majority of cloth worn by enslaved people in Georgia was imported from Great Britain. The letterbooks and correspondence of merchants in Savannah and Charleston are filled with orders for "oznaberg" cloth or other rough textiles for "negroes." Very little cotton was then grown in the low country. When the war shut down the rice trade with England, planters transitioned to cotton as a default crop. Subsequent to this, planters charged slaves with cultivating provisions and cotton for feeding and clothing them. After the Revolution, imports of "Negroe cloth" continued until the explosion in cotton cultivation created a new playing field. Paul Pressley to Jessica Smith, e-mail December 20, 2018.

11 Daniel F. Towles served as subassistant commissioner in the Bureau of Refugees, Freedmen, and Abandoned Lands, also known as the Freedmen's Bureau, in the Summerville, South Carolina, district. While a major part of the bureau's early activities involved the supervision of abandoned and confiscated property, its mission was to provide relief and help freedmen become self-sufficient. See "Records of the Field Offices for the State of South Carolina, Bureau of Refugees, Freedmen, and Abandoned Lands, 1865–1872, Smithsonian Online Virtual Archives, Smithsonian Institution, https://sova.si.edu/record/NMAAHC.FB.M1910, accessed August 5, 2018. "A Story of Land, History and Lowcountry Lifestyle," Martins Point Plantation website, http://martinspointplantation.com/history/, accessed July 25, 2018.

12 According to the Old Slave Mart Museum website, Ryan's Mart (built in 1859 and also known as the Old Slave Mart) is considered the last surviving slave auction gallery in South Carolina: See http://www.oldslavemartmuseum.com/.

13 "Slavery Relics Sought Here for South Carolina Museum," *Mobil Alabama Press-Register*, ca. 1950s, Old Slave Mart Museum Records Collection (acc. 2017-72), Miriam B. Wilson Papers, University of Charleston Special Collections Library, hereafter OSMMRC. As of May 2019, this collection had not been processed.

14 Mrs. Feagin of Macon, Ga., to Miriam Wilson, letter August 9, 1948, OSMMRC.

15 Museum visitor to Miriam B. Wilson, February 28, 1955, OSMMRC.

16 Acacia Collection website, http://acaciacollection.com/ (dead), accessed February 1, 2017.

17 In November 2017, all items from the Acacia Collection, including the OSMM artifacts, were individually auctioned in the Slotkin Folk Art Auction. The auction catalog (see note 2 in this chapter) heralded the auction as containing "The Acacia Collection and The Old Slave Mart Museum, along with the best in Self-Taught Art, Outsider Art, Southern Folk Pottery & Anonymous Folk Art" (front cover). That slave artisanship appears in an auction that bills itself as "The #1 Source for Buying and Selling Self-Taught Art" frames slave work in opposition to the fine arts. (See example in Slotkin promotional materials, https://www.liveauctioneers.com/auctioneer/355/slotin-folk-art/.)

18 *Slotkin Folk Art Auction* catalog, 161.

19 Strip weaving is the most common form of weaving found across West Africa. There are three types of looms at play (single-heddle ground looms, vertical single-heddle looms, and double-heddle narrow-strip loom) with the double-heddle narrow-strip loom dominant in most regions. Weavers were historically male (with the exception of a select group of Nigerian women who utilized vertical looms), though there has been a contemporary movement to educate female weavers. The most well-known African woven textile is kente cloth, woven by the Ashanti and Ewe people of Ghana and Togo. These brightly patterned geometric textiles, and their reproductions, can be seen in African American celebration dress across the United States (Clarke, Gardi, and Sorber 2015, 25). Strip weaving in West Africa can be traced back to the eleventh century, with cotton woven strip fragments found in the Tellum caves from the Bandiagara encampment in Mali. Arab expansion across the Sahara brought Islam along with new forms of dress. Rulers across the region increased textile consumption, supporting the development of a specialized craft practice. When European traders reached the coast of West Africa in the fifteenth century, they found well-established weaving centers and bolts of cloth being distributed as a medium of exchange (Bouttiaux, Sorber, and Van Cutsem 2019, 88).

20 Andrea Feeser (2013, 67) points out that the South Carolina backcountry was settled from 1730 based on subsistence strategies ranging from small homesteads to substantial plantations. Slaves were a vital part of this economy, and by the latter 1770s, two-thirds of slaves in South Carolina were purchased by back country settlers.

21 Paul Rucker, *Rewind*, 2017, York College Art Galleries: York College of Pennsylvania, http://www.rewindexhibition.com/.

22 Staff, Boyhood Home of President Woodrow Wilson, Augusta, Ga., April 2019. See also the museum website, https://www.wilsonboyhoodhome.org/.

23 "About the Boyhood Home of President Woodrow Wilson," https://www.wilsonboyhoodhome.org/learn/about-boyhood-home/, accessed March 19, 2019.

24 Erick Montgomery further clarified the source of these materials, e-mail April 21, 2019.

25 Staff, Liberty Hall, Crawfordville, Ga., August 2016.

26 Lisa Raflo, A. H. Stephens Memorial State Park application for National Register of Historic Places, 1995, p. 10, https://npgallery.nps.gov/GetAsset/b7f1b21e-8cc9-4383-b683-3923650a59f7. The application goes on: "The A. H. Stephens Memorial State Park buildings, structures, objects, and landscaping constructed during the 1930s, and the restoration of the Liberty Hall resources, are historically significant for their association with the social, political, and economic impact of the Great Depression and the subsequent development of the various Federal Relief Programs such as the Civilian Conservation Corps and the Works Progress Administration which were responsible for their construction and restoration. The Civilian Conservation Corps in particular is considered the most popular and successful of these programs and is also considered one of the great conservation programs in the history of the United States" (10–11).

27 Many accounts survive of Stephen's "generosity" to his slaves, later servants. Meanwhile, Stephens is famous for supporting the institution of slavery and for also admitting to its cruelty.

28 See data including table 11, "Agriculture—Farms and Implements, Stock, Products, and Home Manufacture," 1850 Census Report, https://www.census.gov/library/publications/1853/dec/1850a.html. Further examination of this and like reports contain clues about the type of weaving described by Baker. Crawfordville is in Taliaferro County on the northern edge of the Black Belt. Demographic statistics from June 1850 show a population of 2,051 whites, 3,044 enslaved residents, and 51 free blacks. According to the Agriculture Schedule, Taliaferro County was a minor player in handmade manufacture, generating goods valued at $7,819 in comparison to Troup County (home to the Lovelace family), where homemade manufacture yielded $23,702 for the county. These data provisionally suggest that the weaving Baker describes was for use on the farm (e.g., to clothe the enslaved), as opposed to being made to sell in local markets.

Chapter 3 Plain-Style People

1 See Ford 1988 and Owsley 1949 for depictions of the yeomanry in Georgia.

2 Joseph Marie Jacquard, who invented a programmable attachment for the Jacquard loom, was the son of a master silk weaver. This invention is widely recognized as an important milestone in computing history and history of programming in particular. The attachment is a notable example of punched card use for data storage. Later, punched cards (pasteboard cards with holes in predefined positions) were used for data and/or program storage and input for different devices, including the first digital computers and Charles Babbage's Analytical Engine.

3 Sara Muschel, letter to Miriam Wilson, 1956, Old Slave Mart Museum Records Collection (acc. 2017-72), Miriam B. Wilson Papers, University of Charleston Special Collections Library.

4 Clark Johnson to Susan Falls, e-mails December 4, 2013, and January 21, 2014. All subsequent quotations by Clark Johnson are from these e-mails.

5 Sadly, in the twenty-first century the Civil War is still described at times as "the War between the States" or "of Northern Agression." We heard several professionals in the field of southern decorative arts use this language.

6 Mills in Lowell, Massachusetts, wove power-loomed geometric overshot fabric that was sewn into coverlets for distribution throughout the Northeast.

7 The four-harness counterbalance loom is often referred to as a barn loom because it could be disassembled and stored in the barn when not in use. Weaving was a winter activity since less time was spent in the fields (see Alvic 2015).

8 See "Fast and the Fugitive" 2012.

9 Other accounts claim that Boone Hall, 10 miles outside of Charleston in Mount Pleasant, inspired the oak-lined entrance to Ashley Wilkes's Twelve Oaks Plantation in the 1939 film adaptation of Mitchell's *Gone with the Wind* (Susan Myrick was an advisor on set about matters of southern culture; see the From the Archive section in chapter 4). Like the Calloway Plantation, the original wooden farmhouse at Boone Hall was replaced (in 1936) with a columned neoclassical brick mansion (See "Gone with the Wind," Movie-Locations.com, http://www.movie-locations.com /movies/g/Gone-With-The-Wind.php). In *Sweet Home Alabama* from 2002, postwar neoclassical architecture is presented as a relic of the antebellum landscape. That film, filmed in rural Georgia, featured the Oak Hill plantation on the Berry College Campus in Rome, where the original 1847 farmhouse (burned in 1884) was rebuilt in the Greek Revival plantation style.

10 "Callaway Plantation," Washington, Ga., website, http://www.kudcom.com/www/att01.html, accessed August 1, 2018.

11 Among the wealth accumulated by the planter class was gold gleaned from the short-lived gold rush (Swanson 2016). The discovery of gold in Dahlonega and the subsequent removal of the Cherokee had an impact on people-land-goods networks since settlers would have eyed Cherokee-owned plantations through the lens of external markets of both yellow gold and white gold, that is, cotton.

12 Edith Rose, "Introduction to Donation of Coverlets and Quilts," 1995, AHC 2006.21.m5/m2/m10, Textile Collection, Atlanta History Center.

13 See also the Jewell Family Collection (1809–1900), Hargrett Rare Book and Manuscript Library, University of Georgia, Athens.

14 See Midway Museum website, http://www.themidwaymuseum.org/midway-people.html, accessed June 2, 2017.

15 Census documents at K. Torp, "1850 Gordon County Census Slave Schedules," Georgia Genealogy Trails, http://genealogytrails.com/geo/gordon/1850slavescensus.html, and "Gordon County, Georgia: 1850 Census Index," USGenWeb Archives, 1988, http://files.usgwarchives.net/ga/gordon/census/1850/1850indx.txt.

16 The Swepson-Littlefield scandal caused the debt of the state of North Carolina to rise from $15 million to $28 million and impacted western communities that had hoped for infrastructural improvements. See Ora Blackman, *Western North Carolina, Its Mountains and Its People to 1880* (Boone, N.C.: Appalachian Consortium Press, 1977).

Chapter 4 Pioneer Sisters

1 Dale Couch, the curator of decorative arts at the Henry D. Green Center for the Study of the Decorative Arts at the University of Georgia–Athens, suggested we examine this archive. The collection description from the unpublished inventory available on-site at the Georgia Archives reads: "The six Jackson Sisters, daughters of Lewis and Margery C. Jackson, lived between 1847 and 1940 on a 300-acre farm in northern Jones County near Hillsboro, GA. After their father died in the Civil War in 1863, they and their mother assumed operation of the family farm and supported themselves by raising cotton, and hogs, spinning and weaving cloth, and producing various baked and canned goods. The collection contains: a few personal papers and memorandum books by three of the sisters; incoming letters from the Jackson and Carmichael cousins; incoming letters from Georgia friends and those who had emigrated to Louisiana and Texas; medical remedies; legal and business papers; photographs; news clippings;

books; miscellaneous other papers, and person artifacts." Jackson Sisters Family Papers, acc. 1970-0297M, Georgia Archives, hereafter JSFP.

2 As chapter 3 notes, caught between the planters (who aimed to extract maximum profit from commercial agriculture) and landless whites, many yeoman families of Georgia and South Carolina practiced what would come to be known as safety-first agriculture, a calculated blend of subsistence farming and commercial cultivation meant to assure that meals would be on the table year-round (see Ford 1988).

3 There was a 26 percent increase in improved lands in the Upper Piedmont with a 40 percent increase in cotton production after the Civil War (Harper 1922).

4 These same Rousseauian ideals were refracted through a Marxist lens to mobilize the Bolshevik Revolution (1918).

5 The former Jackson homestead is now part of Piedmont National Wildlife Refuge, "Information about the Jackson Sisters," RootsWeb, http://www.rootsweb.ancestry.com/~gajasper/infoabtjackson.htm. More information about the Jasper County Historical Association can be found at their website, http://thomaspersonshall.com.

6 Lewis Jackson was born to John Jackson (of Culpepper, Va., b. 1783) and Mary Pollock Hammock (1700–1842).

7 Staff at the Georgia Archives took the opportunity of our visit to examine and reroll (for better conservation) the few textile artifacts associated with the Jackson Sisters Family Papers (JSFP).

8 The daughter of a planter, Susan Myrick came of age when elite southern society was shifting from raising daughters in the "cult of true womanhood" (pious, pure, submissive, and domestic) to "real womanhood" (athletic, self-sufficient, and educated), allowing (or encouraging) women to work for a living in activities deemed appropriate for women, such as teaching, to be economically independent so that they were not dependent on marriage (see Susan M. Cruea, "Changing Ideals of Womanhood During the Nineteenth-Century Woman Movement," 2005, General Studies Writing Faculty Publications, paper 1 at http://scholarworks.bgsu.edu/gsw_pub/1). Myrick's support of the so-called Lost Cause narrative, wherein elite southern women are viewed as a "civilizing" force, is not unlike the "noble savage" ideology we see reflected in Miriam Wilson's OSMM documents.

9 These documents were difficult for us to read. It is crucial that students continue to be taught how to write and read cursive script so that historical materials such as these remain decipherable.

10 Lillie Malone, Macon, Ga., letter November 5, 1905, JSFP.

11 The flyer Mrs. Payne refers to was not in the collection when we visited in 2015.

12 Ironically, Hubbard's extreme pacifism led to his death in May 1915. As Hubbard explained to Ernest Cowper, a Canadian journalist aboard the *Lusitania*, he wanted to see for himself whether he had been justified in writing "Who Lifted the Lid Off of Hell?," his attack on Kaiser Wilhelm (published in *Philistine*, October 1914, reported in W. Eaton, Read, and Wood 1919). There, Hubbard had denounced the German ruler the "mastoid degenerate of a noble grandmother" as a "War-Lord" who does not represent the "true" Germany; he called for disarmament and a World Federation, observing that "William the Second" has exploded "the bromidial fallacy that vast armaments insure peace" (Hubbard 1914 in Eaton, Read, and Wood 1919). Both Elbert Hubbard and his "periodical of protest" went down with the sinking of the *Lusitania*; many of his readers were convinced that the Kaiser had ordered the ship's sinking in revenge of Hubbard's incendiary comments (White 1986, 88–89).

Chapter 5 An Optical Art

1 We were initially unsure why coverlets were relegated to workaday spaces given the training, effort, and materials required to produce them. The basic facts of the weaving process clearly preclude coverlets from being "make-do" goods.

2 American Fancy is both in association with but ontologically distinct from the notion of fancy as imaginative play outlined by British and Scottish Enlightenment philosophers.

3 The closest thing we saw to a Fancy style was in the Ware-Lyndon master bedroom in Athens, where one coverlet is on the foot of the bed, and the second is placed as an accent on a settee. They are, however, not unfurled.

4 See also discussion of spinning wheels as icons of the colonial revival in Marling 1988.

5 In the first half to the twentieth century, artists, writers, cultural historians, and collectors of modern art set out to establish a U.S. cultural heritage in line with the European modernist strategy of drawing from folk and primitive art practices. Pivotal to this quest were Constance Rourke (editor of the Index of American Design), Holger Cahill (curator at the Museum of Modern Art, and national director of the Federal Art Project), and Edith Halpert (Cahill's business partner and seller of American folk art). Each worked to promote American folk art as the progenitor of modernism (Clayton 2003, 20). Cahill's influential exhibition, *American Folk Art: The Art of the Common Man in America, 1750–1900*, embodied

the populist spirit of the times. Consisting almost entirely of Abby Aldrich Rockefeller's Folk-Art Collection, it was held at the first U.S. museum devoted to modern art: MoMA.

6 Broomfield 2006 explains that by the late nineteenth century, when Frost made his first field trip into the mountain communities, many mountain looms were sitting idle. Craft production was primarily the work of the elder generation of women in the communities; those who had learned to weave from their own mothers were keeping the textile traditions alive. In 1896 and 1897, Frost's annual reports to Berea College trustees articulated his desire to establish an industry that would help students pay their way through college.

7 A folksy, make-do ideology exists even until today, even by educated textile scholars, who asked us why we were interested in these objects, given that coverlet weaving is "just mechanical." Others regarded coverlet weaving as hipster-washed "granny-chic."

8 "Textiles from the Index of American Design," National Gallery of Art, https://www.nga.gov/features/slideshows/textiles-from-the-index-of-american-design.html#slide_3, accessed January 2016. The National Gallery of Art Index of Images contains hand-drawn illustrations of woven coverlets. Ruth Barnes created several of these, and not just with coverlets as a subject. See, for example, the photo of her 1937 *Coverlet* at the National Gallery of Art website, https://www.nga.gov/collection/art-object-page.12816.html.

9 The new looms were based on the traditional counterbalance barn loom with modern mechanical fittings that operated more smoothly, leading to fewer weaving faults resulting from malfunctioning mechanics.

10 The attachment of overshot and Appalachian communities to U.S. nationalism is a striking development given the history of overshot as a technique and style as well as the immigration histories of "mountain folk," both of which fall outside of the scope of this book but are interesting to contemplate in light of the rise of "traditional chic."

11 For a fascinating visual timeline of White House interiors, see "Living Room," White House Museum, http://www.whitehousemuseum.org/floor2/living-room.htm, accessed May 20, 2018.

12 The dominant popular understanding at the time (an idea that persists in some quarters even today) was that societies moved through what anthropologists called unilineal evolution. This is the idea that societies develop along a predetermined path, with urban European society representing the apex of cultural and political development. Franz Boas's historical particularism, which suggested that each society develops along

its own path in response to external political and cultural dynamics, was not as well known as salvage ethnography.

13 In 1931, 1933, and 1938, Halpert and Cahill organized three folk art shows titled *Ancestors of American Art*, providing a visual repertoire of American modernism rooted in the rural past.

14 As one of our external reviewers pointed out, Marianne Brandt was a Bauhaus exception among women; she made it into the metal workshop and produced significant designs.

15 The emergence of the Frankfurt School for Social Research was contemporary with the "objective" phase of the Bauhaus, 1923–33; the ideas and evolution of both the Bauhaus and the Frankfurt School can be understood as symptomatic responses to a fundamental dilemma posed by the "rationalism" of technological modernity (Ockman 2009).

16 Katz 2013 is among the good accounts of the founding and history of Black Mountain College.

17 See images and further information about Laurie Herrick's *Three Giraffes* (1971) at Sarah Margolis-Pineo (2013), *Metamuseum*, May 26, http://metamuseum.tumblr.com/post/51389793234/laurie-herrick-three-giraffes-c-1970-wool. Namita Gupta Wiggers curated an exhibition of Herrick's work, including this piece, at the Museum of Contemporary Craft (2011). See especially Bridget Riley's *Movement in Squares* (1961), tempera on hardboard. Many well-known art works in the op art lineage employ a black and white palette, which was one of the reasons that, when we launched *Fold Unfold* (Falls and Smith 2017a, 2017b) as a way to research overshot, we limited entries to a black-grey-white scheme.

18 See documentation from the Museum of Contemporary Crafts Artists-in-Residence program in which Pam Patrie, Mackenzie Frère, Christy Matson, Elizabeth Whalen, and Deborah Valoma created personal responses to Herrick's patterns, "Laurie Herrick: Weaving Yesterday, Today and Tomorrow," *Flickr*, https://www.flickr.com/photos/contemporarycraft/collections/72157626538476945/. Rosalie Neilson's work can be viewed at her website, https://www.rosalieneilson.com/rep-weave/.

19 See De Young Museum website for further information about the exhibition, https://deyoung.famsf.org/grid-textiles-and-minimalism.

Chapter 6 Unfolded

1 In a 2009 essay, Giorgio Agamben (2009) distinguishes between beings and the apparatuses (schools, laws, computers, agriculture, cigarettes, etc.) that ensnare, orient, and control the gestures, behaviors, opinions and even creations of beings. He introduces a third category of the subject,

which represents the relation between being and apparatus; it is through a process of subjectification that beings capitulate will; subjectification entails the abdication of competence. Conversely, the beginning point of politics is the *ungovernable*, that subject beyond the reach of the apparatus, so it is also a beginning point for reclamation. Not all poetry roughens. Not all painting reveals the conditions of its own production. Not all weaving represents a refusal to abdicate. But poetry, painting, and weaving can work as an everyday political aesthetic that calls attention to the larger forces of power and knowledge against which it exists.

2 The intimate relationship that exists between the aesthetic and the political is often overlooked in analyses of contemporary society. Like two sides of a coin, aesthetic practices and political values and desires act in unity, speaking to identity and aspiration. Insightful analyses of the political aesthetic were developed by members of the Frankfurt School like Theodor Adorno, Max Horkheimer, and Walter Benjamin. A lesser-known associate was Sigfried Kracauer, a film and literature editor at the German newspaper *Fraankfurter Zeitung*. Kracauer thought deeply about how foundational structures of society reverberated through and because of aesthetic activity that had been treated as trivial, or at least derivative, by social theorists (most of whom were in dialogue with Marx). In a 1927 essay, Kracauer lays out how aesthetic phenomena ought to be read: "The position that an epoch occupies in the historical process can be determined more strikingly from an analysis of its inconspicuous surface-level expressions than from that epoch's judgments about itself. Since these judgments are expressions of the tendencies of a particular era, they do not offer conclusive testimony about its overall constitution. The surface-level expressions, however, by virtue of their unconscious nature, provide unmediated access to the fundamental substance of the state of things. Conversely, knowledge of this state of things depends on the interpretation of these surface-level expressions. The fundamental substance of an epoch and its unheeded impulses illuminate each other reciprocally" (Kracauer 1995, 75). Kracauer asks us to look beyond the surface objects such as coverlets to discover their political entailments. Arranged more or less chronologically, this book follows how these objects advance, reflect, critique, or resist relations of power implicated in the conditions of their making. Aesthetic practices and the objects they produce can reproduce the status quo, but they can also assess the conditions of their own creation, opening a space for alternative relations with these conditions. For starters, the inevitable inconsistencies on even expertly handwoven textiles distinguish them from machine-made textiles. The execution of patterns as well as coloration, seam alignment,

and so forth all reflect the hand and skill of the weaver, but also disclose even more: prerequisite values such as color, material, and pattern choice; tools, such as gins, looms, threads, spinning wheels, dye technologies, and agricultural practices; and ideologies surrounding consumption, material culture, labor, gender, identity, and so forth.

3 Political activity that is tacit rather than explicit is extremely potent, working on us in ways that are less than obvious. Scholars of identity have taught us to pay attention to the ways that gender, racial, national, and religious inequalities are produced and maintained.

4 Bluestone 2014, an analysis of deindustrializing America, shows how corporate restructuring has contributed to the unsustainable growth in low-paying jobs and a ballooning of high-wage jobs, but few in the middle. Of course, this has meant a loss of middle-class incomes. Part of this reconfiguration has to do with a shift in production from the manufacturing of hard goods to making highly imaginative, abstract financial, real estate, and insurance products that have little relationship to manufacturing labor.

5 The cultural theorist Walter Benjamin worried about the aestheticization of the political as a move that took the realm of the political, which is always about power and control, and repositioned it as style that lacked depth and was subject to easy manipulation. Jon Simons (2014) argues against the Benjaminian implication advanced in contemporary contexts by thinkers such as David Harvey, Terry Eagleton, and Jürgen Habermas that, because power is aestheticized, the political is necessarily ideological or impoverished. Simons points out that position is based on a restrictive, philosophical, modernist conception of the aesthetic. Reading Nietzsche through Foucault, Simon finds an aesthetics of existence as a step toward elaborating a more appropriate notion of aesthetics. Whereas a modernist construction differentiates aesthetics from politics and ethics as different value spheres, an aesthetics of experience enmeshes the spheres and displaces any fascist connotations of understanding politics aesthetically.

6 The term *textile* is derived from the Latin *texere*, to weave, using a warp and weft: a grid.

7 Digital images, tending toward a glossy homogeneity of palette, line, and composition, use hyperlinks and ready-made elements of weather, "scalies," furniture, and landscape to depict a world snapped to grid.

8 See *Continuous Monument*, Cristiano Toraldo di Francia, https://www.cristianotoraldodifrancia.it/continuous-monument/.

9 See work by Gilles Deleuze and Félix Guatarri (1980), Jaron Lanier (2017), David Harvey (1990).

Bibliography

Agamben, Georgio. 2009. *"What Is an Apparatus?" and Other Essays.* Translated by David Kishik and Stefan Pedatella. Stanford, Calif.: Stanford University Press.

Albers, Anni. 1941. "Handweaving Today: Textile Work at Black Mountain College." *Weaver* 6 (1): 3–7.

Alcott, Louisa May. 1884. *Spinning Stories.* Cambridge: University Press, John Wilson & Son.

Alderman, Derek. N.d. "Tourism RESET: Race, Ethnicity, and Social Equity in Tourism." http://tourismreset.com/.

Alvic, Philis. 2015. *Weavers of the Southern Highlands.* Lexington: University Press of Kentucky.

Ames, Kenneth. 1985. Introduction. In *The Colonial Revival in America*, edited by Alan Axelrod. New York: W. W. Norton.

Anderson, Clarita. 2002. *American Coverlets and Their Weavers: Coverlets from the Collection of Foster and Muriel McCarl.* Williamsburg, Va.: Colonial Williamsburg Foundation, in association with Ohio University Press.

Atlanta History Center and the Madison Morgan Cultural Center. 2006. *Neat Pieces: The Plain-Style Furniture of Nineteenth-Century Georgia.* Athens: University of Georgia Press.

Atwater, Mary. 1941. "It's Pretty—But Is It Art?" *Weaver* 6 (3): 13–14.

Avary, Myrta Lockett, ed. 1910. *Recollections of Alexander H. Stephens: His Diary Kept When a Prisoner at Fort Warren, Boston Harbour, 1865; giving incidents and reflections of his prison life and some letters and reminiscences.* New York: Doubleday.

Baker, Georgia. 1941. "Plantation Life: Interview with Georgia Baker, 369 Meigs Street, Athens, Georgia. Written by Mrs. Sadie B. Hornsby." In Federal Writers' Project, *Slave Narratives*, vol. 4, *Georgia Narratives*, part 1, 37–57. https://memory.loc.gov/mss/mesn/041/041.pdf.

Barber, E. J. W. 2006. *Prehistoric Textiles: The Development of Cloth in the Neolithic and Bronze Ages with Special Reference to the Aegean.* Princeton, N.J.: Princeton University Press.

Batteau, Allen. 1979. "Appalachia and the Concept of Culture: A Theory of Shared Misunderstandings." *Appalachian Journal of Architectural Education* 7 (1979–80): 28.

Bean, Susan. 1990. "The American Market for Indian Textiles, 1785–1820: In the Twilight of Traditional Cloth Manufacture." In *Textiles in Trade*, Proceedings of the Textile Society of America Biennial Symposium, edited by M. Gittinger, 43–52. Los Angeles, Calif.: Textile Society of America.

Bechmann, F. E. 1920. "Dog's Wool." *Dogdom* 21 (1): 5.

Becker, Jane. 1998. *Selling Tradition : Appalachia and the Construction of an American Folk*. Chapel Hill: University of North Carolina Press.

Beckert, Sven. 2015. *Empire of Cotton*. New York: Vintage Books.

Bluestone, Barry. 2014. *The Great U-Turn: Inequality in America Twenty-Five Years Later.* Los Angeles: UCLA Luskin School of Public Affairs. https://luskin.ucla.edu/sites/default/files/bluestone_pres.pdf.

Bourriaud, Nicolas. 2002. *Relational Aesthetics*. Paris: Presses du réel.

Bouttiaux, Anne-Marie, Frieda Sorber, and Anne Van Cutsem. 2019. *African Costumes and Textiles: From the Berbers to the Zulus: The Zaira and Marcel Mis Collection*. Milan: 5 Continents Press.

Bress, Helene. 2003. *The Coverlet Book: Early American Handwoven Coverlets*. Gaithersburg, Md.: Flower Valley Press.

Broomfield, Sarah Stopenhagen. 2006. "Weaving Social Change: Berea College Fireside Industries and Reform in Appalachia." Textile Narratives & Conversions: Proceedings of the 10th Biennial Symposium of the Textile Society of America, October 11–14, Toronto, Ont.

Bruegel, Martin. 2002. *Farm, Shop, Landing: The Rise of a Market Society in the Hudson Valley, 1780–1860*. Durham, N.C.: Duke University Press.

Cardon, Dominique. 2007. *Natural Dyes: Sources, Tradition, Technology and Science*. London: Archetype.

Cascone, Sarah. 2017. "A College Decided that This Anti-Racist Art Show Was Too 'Provocative' for the Public." *ArtNews*, October 13, 2017. https://news.artnet.com/exhibitions/paul-rucker-rewind-york-college-1114256.

Casto, Marilyn. 2006. "Hand Production in Colonial Revival Interiors." In *Re-Creating the American Past*, edited by Richard Guy Wilson, Shaun Eyring, and Kenny Marotta, 321–35. Charlottesville: University of Virginia Press.

Chase, Judith Wragg. 1971. *Afro-American Art and Craft*. New York: Van Nostrand Reinhold.

Clark, Krissy. 2013. "The Middle Class through the Hollywood Lens." *MarketPlace/Wealth and Poverty*, June 28, 2018. https://www.marketplace.org/2013/06/28/wealth-poverty/middle-class-through-hollywood-lens.

Clark, Sonya. 2015. *The Hair Craft Project*. [Richmond, Va.: Sonya Clark.] http://sonyaclark.com/sc_text/the-hair-craft-project, accessed January 10, 2018.

Clarke, Duncan, Berhnard Gardi, and Frieder Sorber. 2015. *African Textiles: The Karun Thakar Collection*. New York: Prestel.

Clayton, Virgina T. 2003. *Drawing on America's Past: Folk Art, Modernism, and the Index of American Design*. Washington, D.C.: National Gallery of Art.

Commission of the Brooklyn and Long Island Fair in Aid of the United States Sanitary. 1864. *History of the Brooklyn and Long Island Fair*. Brooklyn, N.Y.: "The Union" Steam Press.

Compa, Lance. 1987. "So We Have More Jobs—Low-Paid, Part-Time Ones." *Washington Post*, March 15, 1987.

Cook, Clarence. 1878. *The House Beautiful, Essays on Beds and Tables, Stools and Candlesticks*. New York: Scribner, Armstrong.

Corradetti, Claudio. 2002. "The Frankfurt School and Critical Theory." In *Internet Encyclopedia of Philosophy*. http://www.iep.utm.edu/frankfur/.

Cosgrove, Ben. 2014. "Gandhi and His Spinning Wheel: The Story Behind an Iconic Photo." *Time*, September 10, 2014. http://time.com/3639043/gandhi-and-his-spinning-wheel-the-story-behind-an-iconic-photo/, accessed January 10, 2015.

Craig, Gabriel. 2010. "Altruism, Activism, and the Moral Imperative in Craft." MFA thesis, Virginia Commonwealth University, 2009.

Davidson, Jan. 1989. Introduction. In *Mountain Homespun: A Facsimilie of the Original, Published in 1931*, edited by Frances Louisa Goodrich. Knoxville: University of Tennessee Press.

Davidson, William H. 1971. *Brooks of Honey and Butter: Plantations and People of Meriwether County, Georgia*. Alexander City, Ala.: Outlook.

Davis, Ben. 2010. "The Bauhaus in History: What Does the Bauhaus Mean to Us, Today?" Artnet, http://www.artnet.com/magazineus/reviews/davis/bauhaus1-28-10.asp, accessed 2019.

Deleuze, Gilles, and Félix Guattari. 1968. *Kafka: Toward a Minor Literature*. Minneapolis: University of Minnesota Press.

Deleuze, Gilles, and Félix Guattari. 1987. *A Thousand Plateaus*. Translated by Brian Massumi. Minneapolis: University of Minnesota Press.

Deleuze, Gilles, Félix Guattari, and Robert Brinkley. 1983. "What Is a Minor Literature?" *Mississippi Review* 11 (3): 13–33.

Desrosiers, S. 2012. "Can We Study Textiles from Other Cultures without Ethnocentrism? The Andes as a Case Study." Paper presented at the Textile Society of America Symposium, September 18–22, 2012. Washington, D.C.

Dormer, Peter. 1997. *The Culture of Craft*. Manchester: Manchester University Press.

Douglass, Frederick. 1845. *Narrative of the Life of Frederick Douglass, An American Slave*. Boston: Anti-Slavery Office.

Durham, Tempie Herndon. 1941. "Tempie Herndon Durham: Ex-Slave 103 Years Old, 1312 Pine St., Durham, N.C. Interviewed by Travis Jordan." In Federal Writers' Project, *Slave Narratives*, vol. 11, *North Carolina Narratives*, part 1, 284–90. https://memory.loc.gov/mss/mesn/111/111.pdf.

Eaton, Allen. 1937. *Handicrafts of the Southern Highlands: With an account of the rural handicraft movement in the United States and suggestions for the wider use of handicrafts in adult education and in recreation*. New York: Russell Sage.

Eaton, William Dunseath, Harry C. Read, and Leonard Wood. 1919. *A Complete History of the World War: A Connected and Complete Narrative of the War on All Fronts, Covering All Events between 1914 and 1924*. Vol. 1. C. Thomas.

Eberlein, Harold D. 1914. "Early Decorative Weaving in America: A Cottage Craft Now Being Revived." *Arts and Decoration (1910–1918)* 4 (11): 414–17.

Eelman, B. W. 2008. *Entrepreneurs in the Southern Upcountry: Commercial Culture in Spartanburg 1845–1880*. Athens: University of Georgia Press.

Eisenstadt, Peter, ed. 2005. *Encyclopedia of New York State*. Syracuse: Syracuse University Press.

Escott, P. 1985. *Many Excellent People: Power and Privilege in North Carolina, 1850–1900*. Chapel Hill: University of North Carolina Press.

Falls, Susan. 2017. *White Gold: Stories of Breast Milk Sharing*. Lincoln: University of Nebraska Press.

Falls, Susan, and Jessica Smith. 2009. "Aesthetic Value of Ikat Textiles." Paper presented at American Anthropological Association Annual Conference, Philadelphia, Pa., December 2–6, 2009.

Falls, Susan, and Jessica Smith. 2010. "The Role of Ethnography in Art and Design " Paper presented at Southeastern College Art Conference (SECAC), Richmond, Va., October 20–23, 2010.

Falls, Susan, and Jessica Smith. 2011. "Branding Authenticity: Cambodian Ikat in Transnational Artisan Partnerships (TAPS)." *Journal of Design History* 24 (3): 255–71.

Falls, Susan, and Jessica Smith. 2013. "Public Art/Art Publics." *Anthropology Now* 5 (1): 67–84.

Falls, Susan, and Jessica Smith. 2017a. *Fold Unfold: An Installation*. Lyndon Ware Arts Center, Athens, Ga., June 24 to August 19, 2017.

Falls, Susan, and Jessica Smith. 2017b. *Fold Unfold: A Project by Susan Falls and Jessica Smith.* Exhibition catalog. N.p.: [CreateSpace].

"The Fast and the Fugitive: Pokeberry Edition." 2012. *Grackle and Sun.* https://grackleandsun.wordpress.com/2012/12/07/the-fast-and-the-fugitive-pokeberry-edition/.

Federal Writers' Project of the Works Progress Administration. 1941. *Slave Narratives: A Folk History of Slavery in the United States from Interviews with Former Slaves.* 17 vols. Washington, D.C.: Library of Congress. Collected 1936–38.

Feeser, Andrea. 2013. *Red, White, and Black Make Blue: Indigo in the Fabric of Colonial South Carolina Life.* Athens: University of Georgia Press.

Felton, Rebecca Latimer. 1919. *Country Life in Georgia in the Days of My Youth (Lived 1835–1930).* Atlanta, Ga.: Index Printing Company.

Fenlon, Paul E. 1954. "The Notorious Swepson-Littlefield Fraud: Railroad Financing in Florida, 1868–1871." *Florida Historical Quarterly* 32 (4): 231–61.

Ferleger, L. A., and J. D. Metz. 2014. *Cultivating Success in the South: Farm Households in the Postbellum Era.* New York: Cambridge University Press.

Fleming, Victor, dir. 1939. *Gone with the Wind.* Warner Brothers.

Ford, Lacy. 1988. *Origins of Southern Radicalism: The South Carolina Upcountry, 1800–1860.* New York: Oxford University Press.

Fox-Genovese, E. 1988. *Within the Plantation Household: Black and White Women of the Old South.* Chapel Hill: University of North Carolina Press.

Fry, Gladys-Marie. 1990. *Stitched from the Soul: Slave Quilts from the Ante-Bellum South.* New York: Dutton Studio Books, in association with the Museum of American Folk Art.

Gardner, Sarah. 2006. *Blood and Irony: Southern White Women's Narratives of the Civil War, 1861–1937.* Chapel Hill: University of North Carolina Press.

Garey, Elisha Doc. 1941. "Plantation Life as Viewed by Ex-Slave Elisha Doc Garey, 258 Lyndon Avenue, Athens, Georgia. Written by Sadie B. Hornsby." In Federal Writers' Project, *Slave Narratives*, vol. 4, *Georgia Narratives*, part 2, 1–10. https://memory.loc.gov/mss/mesn/042/042.pdf.

Georgia Writers' Project. 1940. *Georgia: A Guide to Its Towns and Countryside.* Athens: University of Georgia Press, sponsored by the Georgia Board of Education.

Gillespie, Michele. 2004. *Free Labor in an Unfree World: White Artisans in Slaveholding Georgia, 1789–1860.* Athens: University of Georgia Press.

Gordon, Beverly. 1998. "Spinning Wheels, Samplers, and the Modern Priscilla: The Images and Paradoxes of Colonial Revival Needlework." *Winterthur Portfolio* 33 (2/3): 163–94.

———. 2014. *Textiles: The Whole Story: Uses, Meanings, Significance.* New York: Thames & Hudson.

Green, Alice. 1941. "Plantation Life as Viewed by Ex-Slave Alice Green, Athens, Georgia. Written by Corry Fowler." In Federal Writers' Project, *Slave Narratives*, vol. 4, *Georgia Narratives*, part 2, 32–37. https://memory.loc.gov/mss/mesn/042/042.pdf.

Greene, Isaiah (Isaac). 1941a. "An Opinion of Slavery by Isaiah Green—Ex-Slave. Submitted by Minnie B. Ross." In Federal Writers' Project, *Slave Narratives*, vol. 4, *Georgia Narratives*, part 2, 48–56. https://memory.loc.gov/mss/mesn/042/042.pdf.

———. 1941b. "The Experiences of an Ex-Slave: Isaac (Isaiah) Greene. By Edwin Driskell." in Federal Writers' Project, *Slave Narratives*, vol. 4, *Georgia Narratives*, part 2, 57–59. https://memory.loc.gov/mss/mesn/042/042.pdf.

Greer, Betsy. 2008. *Knitting for Good!* Berkeley, Calif.: Trumpeter.

Griffin, Heard. 1941. "An Interview with Heard Griffin, Ex-Slave. By Minnie B. Ross." In Federal Writers' Project, *Slave Narratives*, vol. 4, *Georgia Narratives*, part 2, 72–77. https://memory.loc.gov/mss/mesn/042/042.pdf.

Griffin, Richard W. 1961. "An Origin of the New South: The South Carolina Homespun Company, 1808–1815." *Business History Review* 35 (3): 402–14.

Grimes, Millard B. 1985. *The Last Linotype: The Story of Georgia and Its Newspapers since World War II.* Macon, Ga.: Mercer University Press.

Gullins, David Goodman. 1941. "Reminiscenses of Slavery Days." In Federal Writers' Project, *Slave Narratives*, vol. 4, *Georgia Narratives*, part 2, 78–90. https://memory.loc.gov/mss/mesn/042/042.pdf.

Hahn, Steven. 1985. "The Unmaking of the Southern Yoemanry." In *The Countryside in the Age of Capitalist Transformation: Essays in the Social History of Rural America*, edited by Steven Hahn and Jonathan Prude, 179–204. Chapel Hill: University of North Carolina Press.

———. 2006. *The Roots of Southern Populism: Yeoman Farmers and the Transformation of the Georgia Upcountry, 1850–1890.* New York: Oxford University Press.

Hall, Eliza Calvert. 1912. *A Book of Hand-Woven Coverlets.* Boston: Little, Brown.

"Hand-Woven Coverlets." 1922. *Bulletin of the Pennsylvania Museum* 18 (72): 16, 19. https://doi.org/10.2307/3794027.

Harmon, Jane Smith Hill. 1941. "Jane Smith Hill Harmon of Washington-Wilkes. By Minnie Branham Stonestreet." In Federal Writers' Project, *Slave Narratives*, vol. 4, *Georgia Narratives*, part 2, 98–102. https://memory.loc.gov/mss/mesn/042/042.pdf.

Harper, Roland. 1922. "Development of Agriculture in Georgia from 1850 to 1920: A Series of Four Articles." *Georgia Historical Quarterly* 6 (1–4): 3–27.

Harris, Dosia. 1941. "Plantation Life as Viewed by Ex-Slave Dosia Harris, 159 Valley Street, Athens, Georgia. Written by Sadie B. Hornsby." In Federal Writers' Project, *Slave Narratives*, vol. 4, *Georgia Narratives*, part 2, 103–14. https://memory.loc.gov/mss/mesn/042/042.pdf.

Harris, Middleton, comp. 1974. *Black Book*. New York: Random House.

Harvey, David. 1990. *The Condition of Postmodernity: An Enquiry into the Origins of Cultural Change*. Cambridge, Mass.: Blackwell.

———. 2005. *A Brief History of Neoliberalism*. Oxford: Oxford University Press.

Jackson, Amanda. 1941. "Ex-Slave Interview: Mrs. Amanda Jackson." In Federal Writers' Project, *Slave Narratives*, vol. 4, *Georgia Narratives*, part 2, 289–93. https://memory.loc.gov/mss/mesn/042/042.pdf.

Jackson, Easter. 1941. "Life Story as Told by Aunt Easter Jackson, Ex-Slave." In Federal Writers' Project, *Slave Narratives*, vol. 4, *Georgia Narratives*, part 2, 299–302. https://memory.loc.gov/mss/mesn/042/042.pdf.

Jensen, Joan M. 1988. *Loosening the Bonds: Mid-Atlantic Farm Women, 1750–1850*. New Haven, Conn.: Yale University Press.

Jentleson, Katherine. 2013. "'Not as Rewarding as the North': Holger Cahill's Southern Folk Art Expedition." *Archives of American Art Journal* (Smithsonian). https://www.aaa.si.edu/publications/essay-prize/2013-essay-prize-katherine-jentleson.

Jones, Robert Sparrow. 2015. "Sonya Clark—Coiffed, Tangled: 'The Hair Craft Project.'" *Michigan Quarterly Review*, February 9, 2015. http://www.michiganquarterlyreview.com.

Joseph, Joseph W., Theresa M. Hamby, and Catherine S. Long. 2004. *Historical Archaeology in Georgia*. University of Georgia Laboratory of Archaeology Series, report 39. https://archaeology.uga.edu/archlab/lab-series/39.

Katz, Vincent. 2013. *Black Mountain College: Experiment in Art*. Boston: MIT Press.

Keller, Patricia J. 1988. "Book Review: Quilts, Coverlets, and Counterpanes: Bedcoverings from the Museum of Early Southern Decorative Arts and Old Salem Collections." *Winterthur Portfolio* 33 (1): 99–103.

Kemble, Fanny. 1961/1984. *Journal of a Residence on a Georgian Plantation in 1838–1839*. Athens: University of Georgia Press.

Kersey, Terrence Lee. 2009. “A Small Place in Georgia: Yeoman Cultural Persistance.” MA thesis, Georgia State University.

———. 2017. “Upcountry Yeoman in Antebellum Georgia: A Comparative Analysis.” PhD diss., Georgia State University.

Koch, Robert. 1967. “Elbert Hubbard’s Roycrofters as Artist-Craftsmen.” *Winterthur Portfolio* 3: 67–82.

Koolhaas, Rem. 1978. *Delirious New York: A Retroactive Manifesto for Manhattan*. New York: Monacelli Press.

Koplos, Janet, and Bruce Metcalf. 2010. *Makers: A History of American Studio Craft*. Chapel Hill: University of North Carolina Press.

Kracauer, Sigfried. 1995. “The Mass Ornament.” In *The Mass Ornament: Weimar Essays*, 74–86. Translated, edited, and introduced by Thomas Y. Levin. Cambridge, Mass.: Harvard University Press.

Krauss, Rosalind. 1965. “Grids.” *October* 9: 50–64.

Krom, Carol. 2003a. “A History of Round Oak.” *History Notes: Jones County History & Heritage, Inc.* (newsletter) 1: 1, 2–3.

———. 2003b. “The Jackson Sisters.” *History Notes: Jones County History & Heritage, Inc.* (newsletter) 1: 1, 3.

Kytle, Ethan J., and Blain Roberts. 2018. *Denmark Vesey’s Garden: Slavery and Memory in the Cradle of the Confederacy*. New York: New Press. Kindle.

La Cour, Erin. 2016. “Comics as a Minor Literature.” *Image and Narrative* 17 (4): 79–90.

Lacques, Anthony. 2006. “Cotton.” *Modern Marvels*. Aired January 18, 2006, on the History Channel.

Lampert, Nicolas. 2014. *A People’s Art History of the United States: 250 Years of Activist Art and Artists Working in Social Justice Movements*. New York: New Press.

Lanier, Jaron. 2017. *Dawn of the New Everything: Encounters with Reality and Virtual Reality*. New York: Henry Holt.

Lester-Makin, Alexandra. 2016. “The Front Tells the Story, the Back Tells the History: A Technical Discussion of the Embroidering of the Bayeux Tapestry.” In *Making Sense of the Bayeux Tapestry: Readings and Reworkings*, edited by Anna Henderson and Gale Owen-Crocker, 23–41. Manchester: Manchester University Press.

Levin, Kevin, ed. 2017. *Interpreting the Civil War at Museums and Historic Sites Interpreting History Series*. New York: Rowman & Littlefield.

Levine, Faythe. 2008. *Handmade Nation: The Rise of DIY, Art, Craft, and Design*. Princeton, N.J.: Princeton Architectural Press.

Lindsley, Susan. 2011. *Susan Myrick of Gone with the Wind: An Autobiographical Biography*. Atlanta: Thomas Max.

Malarcher, Patricia. 1985. "Anni Albers and the Thread of Art." *New York Times*, August 25, 1985, CN11.

Malone, Ann Patton. 1986. "Piney Woods Farmers of South Georgia, 1850–1900: Jeffersonian Yeomen in an Age of Expanding Commercialism." *Agricultural History* 60 (4): 51–84.

Marks, Paula Mitchell. 1996. *Hands to the Spindle: Texas Women and Home Textile Production, 1822–1880*. College Station: Texas A&M University Press.

Marling, Karal Anne. 1988. *George Washington Slept Here: Colonial Revivals and American Culture, 1860–1986*. Cambridge, Mass.: Harvard University Press.

Marx, Karl. 1973. "The Fragment on Machines." In *Grundrisse: Foundations of the Critique of Political Economy*, 690–712. Translated by Martin Nicolaus. New York: Penguin.

McCarl, Foster, and Clarita Anderson. 2002. *American Coverlets and Their Weavers: Coverlets from the Collection of Foster and Muriel Mccarl: Including a Dictionary of More than 700 Weavers*. Williamsburg, Va.: Colonial Williamsburg Foundation.

McCurry, Stephanie. 1992. "The Politics of Yeoman Households." In *Divided Houses: Gender and the Civil War*, edited by Catherine Clinton and Nina Silber, 22–41. New York: Oxford University Press.

———. 1995. *Masters of Small Worlds: Yeoman Households, Gender Relations and the Political Culture of the Antebellum South Carolina Low Country*. New York: Oxford University Press.

McMillen, Sally G. 2002/1992. *Southern Women: Black and White in the Old South*. 2nd ed. Wheeling, Ill.: Harland Davidson.

Meyers, Christopher C. 2008. *The Empire State of the South: Georgia History in Documents and Essays*. Macon, Ga.: Mercer University Press.

Miller, Barbara, and Deb Schillo, eds. 2014. *Frances L. Goodrich's Brown Book of Weaving Drafts*. Atglen, Pa.: Schiffer.

Minca, Laura. 2012. "Rem Koolhaas: Delirious New York: A Retroactive Manifesto for Manhattan (1978)." *Architecture + Urbanism*. http://architectureandurbanism.blogspot.com/2012/02/rem-koolhaas-delirious-new-york-1978.html.

Mitchell, Margaret. 1936. *Gone with the Wind*. New York: Macmillan.

Murphy, Reg. 1957. "Tribute to Susan Myrick." *Macon Telegraph*, July 10, 1957.

Myrick, Susan. 1929. "Five Sisters Lead Pioneer Lives." Lifestyle, Sunday magazine, *Macon Telegraph*, May 6, 1929, 3-6.

———. 1969. "Looking Back: Jackson Girls." *Macon Telegraph*, April 10, 1969.

Nayer, Pramod. 2010. *Contemporary Literary and Cultural Theory: From Structuralism to Ecocriticism*. Delhi, India: Longman Pearson.

O'Reilly, Dougald J. W. 2003. "Further Evidence of Heterarchy in Bronze Age Thailand." *Current Anthropology* (44): 300–306.

Oberg, Charlotte. 1994. "Fra Elbertus and the Roycrofters: Medievalism in East Aurora." In *Medievalism in North America*, edited by Kathleen Verduin, 69–84. Rochester, N.Y.: D. S. Brewer.

Ockman, Joan. 2009. "Object Lessons from the Bauhaus." *Art in America* December (1). http://www.artinamericamagazine.com/news-features/magazine/object-lessons-from-the-bauhaus/.

Olmsted, Frederick Law. 1856. *A Journey in the Seaboard Slave States with Remarks on their Economy*. London: Samson Low, Son.

———. 1861. *The Cotton Kingdom*. New York: Mason Brothers.

O'Sullivan, Simon. 2009. "From Stuttering and Stammering to the Diagram: Deleuze, Bacon and Contemporary Art Practice." *Journal of Deleuze Studies* 3 (2): 247–58.

Owsley, Frank Lawrence. 1949. *Plain Folk of the Old South*. Baton Rogue: Louisiana State University Press.

Peck, Amelia. 1990. *American Quilts and Coverlets in the Metropolitan Museum of Art*. New York: Metropolitan Museum of Art.

Pederson, Ann. 1978. "Georgia Archive VI, Issue 2." *Georgia Archive* 6 (2): 1–89. https://digitalcommons.kennesaw.edu/georgia_archive/vol6/iss2/12.

Petersens, Magnus Af. 2014. "The Visual Poetry of Richard Tuttle." In *Richard Tuttle: I Don't Know. The Weave of Textile Language*, 73–81. Exhibition catalog. London: Tate.

Pollard, E. A. (1867). *The Lost Cause: A New Southern History of the War of the Confederates*. Baltimore, Md.: E. B. Treat.

Pressly, Paul M. 2013. *On the Rim of the Caribbean: Colonial Georgia and the British Atlantic World*. Athens: University of Georgia Press.

Priddy, Sumpter T. 2004. *American Fancy: Exuberance in the Arts, 1790–1820*. Milwaulkee, Wis.: Milwaulkee Art Museum.

Pryor, Joseph. 1851. "Joseph Pryor's Will." September 22, 1851. User Home Page Genealogy Report: Ancestors of Martha Nancy Allen, Genealogy.com. http://www.genealogy.com/ftm/k/e/l/Richard-Kelly/GENE9-0007.html.

Ramsey, Bets, and Merikay Waldvogel. 1998. *Southern Quilts: Surviving Relics of the Civil War*. Nashville, Tenn: Rutledge Hill Press.

Rancière, Jacques. 2010. *Dissensus: On Politics and Aesthetics*. New York: Continuum.

Reidy, Joseph. 1992. *From Slavery to Agrarian Capitalism in the Cotton Plantation South: Central Georgia, 1800–1880*. Chapel Hill: University of North Carolina Press.

Rigley, Ida. "Ida Rigley, Forrest City, Arkansas. Interviewed by Miss Irene Robertson." In Federal Writers' Projcct, *Slave Narratives*, vol. 2, *Arkansas Narratives*, part 6, 42–46. https://memory.loc.gov/mss/mesn/026/026.pdf.

Rourke, Constance. 2003. "Picturing a Usable Past." In *Drawing on America's Past: Folk Art, Modernism, and the Index of American Design*, edited by Virginia Tuttle Clayton, 1–45. Washington, D.C.: National Gallery of Art.

Ruskin, John. 1849. *The Seven Lamps of Architecture*. London: Smith, Elder.

———. 1851. *The Nature of Gothic*. London: Smith, Elder.

Safford, Carleton L., and Robert Bishop. 1987. *America's Quilts and Coverlets*. New York: Random House Value.

Sartwell, Crispin. 2010. *Political Aesthetics*. Ithaca, N.Y.: Cornell University Press.

Scott, Anne Firor. 1995. *Southern Lady: From Pedestal to Politics, 1830–1930*. Charlottesville: University Press of Virginia.

Scott, Mollie Hardy. "Mollie Hardy Scott; R.F.D., DeValls Bluff, Arkansas. Interviewed by Miss Irene Robertson." In Federal Writers' Project, *Slave Narratives*, vol. 2, *Arkansas Narratives*, part 6, 128–30. https://memory.loc.gov/mss/mesn/026/026.pdf.

Shaw, Madelyn. (2012). "Slave Cloth and Clothing Slaves: Craftsma-nship, Commerce, and Industry." *MESDA Journal of Early Southern Decorative Arts* 37. http://www.mesdajournal.org/2012/slave-cloth-clothing-slaves-craftsmanship-commerce-industry/.

———, and Lynne Zacek Bassett. 2012. *Homefront and Battlefield: Quilts and Context in the Civil War*. Lowell, Mass.: American Textile History Museum.

Shaw, Stephanie. 2003. "Using the WPA Ex-Slave Narratives to Study the Impact of the Great Depression." *Journal of Southern History* 69 (3): 623–58.

Sherwin, Brian. 2007. "Art Space Talk: Julian Stanczak." *Myartspace* (blog), July 23, 2007. http://myartspace-blog.blogspot.com/2007/07/art-space-talk-julian-stanczak.html.

Silverstein, Jason. 2018. "The Persistence of Whitewashing: How Can Americans Have Such Different Memories of Slavery?" *New Republic*, May

31, 2018. https://newrepublic.com/article/148618/persistence-whitewashing.

Simons, Jon. 2014. "Benjamin's Communist Idea: Aestheticized Politics, Technology, and the Rehearsal of Revolution." *European Journal of Political Theory* 15 (1): 43–60.

Slay. 2001. *Georgia Civil War Manuscript Collections: An Annotated Bibliography*. Tuscaloosa: University of Alabama Press.

Soffer, Olga, James M. Adovasio, and D. C. Hyland. 2000. "The 'Venus' Figurines: Textiles, Basketry, Gender, and Status in the Upper Paleolithic." *Current Anthropology* 41 (4): 511–37.

Speer, Jean Haskell. 1989. "Woodpiles and Haystacks: Alan Eaton's Vision of Southern Highland Handicrafts." *Southern Folklore* 46: 255–64.

Spivak, Gayatri. 1988. "Can the Subaltern Speak?" In *Marxism and the Interpretation of Culture*, edited by C. Nelson and L. Grossberg, 271–313. Basingstroke, UK: Macmillan Education.

Staples, Kathleen A., and Madeyln Shaw. 2013. *Clothing through American History: The British Colonial Era*. Santa Barbara, Calif.: Greenwood.

Star, Susan. 1999. "The Ethnography of Infrastructure." *American Behavioral Scientist* 43 (4): 377–91.

———, and James R. Griesemer. 1989. "Institutional Ecology, 'Translations,' and Boundary Objects: Amateurs and Professionals in Berkeley's Museum of Vertebrate Zoology, 1907–1939." *Social Studies of Science* 19: 387–420.

Stavisky, Leonard Price. 1949. "Negro Craftmanship in Early America." *American Historical Review* 54 (2): 315–25.

Stoddart, Jess. 2002. *Challenge and Change in Appalachia: The Story of Hindman Settlement School*. Lexington: University Press of Kentucky.

Stone-Ferrier, Linda. 1991. "Spun Virtue, the Lacework of Folly, and World Wound Upside-Down: Seventeenth-Century Dutch Depictions of Female Handwork." In *Cloth and Human Experience*, edited by Annette B. Weiner and Jane Schneider, 215–42. Washington, D.C.: Smithsonian Books.

Strickler, Carol. 1987. *American Woven Coverlets*. Loveland, Colo.: Interweave.

Swanson, D. 2016. "From Georgia to California and Back: The Rise, Fall, and Rebirth of Southern Gold Mining." *Georgia Historical Quarterly* 100 (2): 160–86.

Syjuco, Stephanie. N.d. "Pattern Migration." Stephanie Syjuco. https://www.stephaniesyjuco.com/projects/pattern-migration, accessed April 8, 2017.

Thompson, Hattie. "Hattie Thompson, Widener, Arkansas. Interviewed by Miss Irene Robertson." In Federal Writers' Project, *Slave Narratives*, vol. 2,

Arkansas Narratives, part 6, 315–17. https://memory.loc.gov/mss/mesn/026/026.pdf.

Tice, Karen. 1998. "School-Work and Mother-Work: The Interplay of Maternalism and Cultural Politics in the Educational Initiatives of Kentucky Settlement Workers, 1910–1930." *Journal of Appalachian Studies* 4 (2): 191–224.

Tobin, Jacqueline L., and Raymond G. Dobard. 1999. *Hidden in Plain View: The Secret Story of Quilts and the Underground Railroad.* New York: Doubleday.

Ulrich, Laurel Thatcher. 2002. *The Age of Homespun: Objects and Stories in the Creation of an American Myth.* New York: Vintage.

Vannini, Phillip, and Jonathan Taggart. 2015. *Off the Grid: Re-assembling Domestic Life.* New York: Routledge.

Van-Tassel, Kristin. 2002. "Nineteenth-Century American Antebellum Literature: The Yeoman Becomes a Country Bumpkin." *American Studies* 43 (1): 51–73.

Vlach, John Michael. 1990/1978. *The Afro-American Tradition in Decorative Arts.* Athens: University of Georgia Press.

———. 1991. *By the Work of Their Hands: Studies in Afro-American Folklife.* Charlottesville: University Press of Virginia.

———. 2004. "The Plantation Landscape." In *American Architectural History: A Contemporary Reader*, edited by Keith Eggener, 95–112. London: Routledge.

Weingarden, Lauren S. 1985. "Aesthetics Politicized: William Morris to the Bauhaus." *Journal of Architectural Education* 38 (3): 8–13.

Weltge, Sigrid Wortmann. 1993. *Women's Work: Textile Art from the Bauhaus.* New York: Chronicle.

Wetherington, Mark V. 2005. *Plain Folk's Fight: The Civil War and Reconstruction in Piney Woods Georgia.* Chapel Hill: University of North Carolina Press.

Whisnant, David E. 2009. *All That Is Native and Fine: The Politics of Culture in an American Region.* Chapel Hill: University of North Carolina Press.

White, Bruce A. 1986. "Elbert Hubbard and 'The Philistine: A Periodical of Protest (1895–1915): The Muscular Journalism of an American Freethinker." *Victorian Periodicals Review* 19 (3): 83–89.

Wilson, Laurel E. Janke. 1986. "Textile Production in Nineteenth Century Orange, Alamance, and Durham Counties, North Carolina." PhD diss., University of North Carolina, Greensboro.

Wilson, Woodrow. 1911. "Address of Governer Wilson." *Berea Quarterly* 15 (1): 24.

Wragg Chase, Judith. 1971. *Afro-American Art and Craft*. New York: Van Nostrand Reinhold.

Wray, Matt. 2006. *Not Quite White: White Trash and the Boundaries of Whiteness*. Durham, N.C.: Duke University Press.

Zonger, Melinda, cur. 2002. *Coverlets and the Spirit of America: The Shein Coverlets*. Atglen, Pa.: Schiffer.

Index